Life at 360°

going full circle to find simplicity

written by Lori Colt
in collaboration with Michael Roach

Elise,
Go for it all
in life!
Simplicity, love,
happiness and fun.

Big Hugs,
Lori

Life at 360°

Dedicated to the one I love, my husband Mike who has survived all these crazy adventures with me, and then relived them again as I wrote this book. Mike contributed greatly to the content of this book through our joint recollections and recounts. And to all our wonderful furry companions—present and past—they have inspired us and have given us enough fodder for a lifetime.

We'd also like to call out both of our families who have given us so much love and support all these years. And to our friends, who know us well and yet still think pretty highly of us—thanks!

This is a true story. Some of the names have been changed but most will know who they are.

*****

Life at 360°

Prologue

We'll start at the beginning, even though the path is one big orbital circle and the steps lead us right back to where we started. In the pursuit of happiness and freedom we had to take a journey to find that often life is perfect just as it is, before we go and complicate everything with our acquisitions, expenditures, and lofty quests.

More often it is the simplest of things and experiences that bring the greatest joys. By letting go of the material stuff, the ladder climbing, and the debt we can reach satisfaction by being grateful for all we have and for those we love in our lives.

When what we have is enough, we are satisfied. It is then that we own our own hearts, our souls, and ourselves.

We wish each and every one who reads our story the same—a happy, carefree, simple, loving and fulfilled life.

*****

Life at 360°

One

The Guy in the Neon Shorts

In 1993, I am in my early thirties. I have been divorced for a few years from an "I married way too young in life man" and things just didn't work out as either of us had planned. I am not dating anyone special at the moment and am living roommate-free at the beach with my two wonderful cats, Rally and Mahalo. I live in the Southern California coastal community of Crown Point in San Diego County. It's a cool beachy community full of suntans, rollerbladers and bougainvilleas. The weather is perfect everyday and the birds are always singing. What I am saying is this place is sweet.

When I am not toiling at my anxiety-producing corporate job that is loveless but pays the bills, or participating in aerobic dance at the gym near my home, I am usually outside walking, running or cycling. I am obsessed with being outdoors in the fresh air and sunshine, as well as with movement. I often do my laundry, grocery shopping and housekeeping late at night after work just so I can free up my weekends to leave early on a Saturday or Sunday morning and spend the day walking along the luminous coastline.

One day in July, I have packed my daypack with fruit, water and a book and I walk eight miles to La Jolla Cove, a lovely protected marine sanctuary that teams with rays, garibaldi, yellowtail, seals, and other fascinating sea life. The plan is to relax when I get to the cove for a few hours, read my book, and then take my time enjoying the scenery on the return trip. While standing on the cove's edge watching athletic men and extremely fit women plunge into the cold sea for an invigorating mile swim to the buoys, I spy a shirtless, tan, young guy in neon green shorts looking my way and smiling. I could swear he is one of my coworkers, a guy named Jim, so I smile and wave back, only to realize I am mistaken—I have no idea who this guy is. I stop waving, turn crimson with embarrassment, do a 180 and walk quickly away pretending like that didn't just happen.

I find a bench a few minutes later when I'm sure I am out of his range and I sit. I start popping grapes into my mouth when the neon green shorts guy rides up on his bike and says, "hi." Then he asks me if I would like to go out for a margarita. I have to laugh, since it is only 11:00 in the morning.

We talk for a while and I instantly like this guy. He carries himself with a fun, free and easy demeanor and I feel immediately disarmed. His name is Mike and he tells me he lives and works right here, in La Jolla. He says he would like to take me out to dinner some Friday night if I am free and then he tells me exactly where he works, and says, "come by sometime." So a few days later I do.

He is actually working at Taco Bell as a manager so I think, "hmmmm, ok, this will be fun. Nice guy but I am not going to expect too much from this." We are at the complete opposite ends of the corporate ladder but "what the heck," I say to myself, "it will be just for kicks and I love a good laugh."

The following Friday, Mike appears at my front door as promised to take me out for dinner. He arrives in his little blue Pontiac LeMans, dressed like Don Johnson from the 1980's television show Miami Vice with a lilac shirt, light colored sport coat and jeans. He is chewing gum and wearing high-top white sneakers with the laces undone. We go out to a restaurant called the Old Town Mexican Café and indulge in cheesy enchiladas along with on-the-rocks margaritas laden with ample tequila. We have a wonderful time. We drink *a lot* of margaritas and then he takes me to a swanky high rise hotel downtown San Diego for more cocktails and a view of the city and harbor skyline from their top story bar. I like this guy. He is delightful and confident, but equally kind and funny as hell. Then gives me the old lip lock and I am even more smitten.

A few weeks into dating, Mike shows up with this long, heavy box and a grin on his face. I have a bunch of music in the form of compact discs and it's all in stacks on a shelf and on the floor. Mike's gift is a CD holder. I'm thinking, "wow," no guy has ever brought me furniture as a gift. He must really like me.

We have a fun courtship. No games. Steady. Fun. The first Friday night date turns into the next Thursday, and then the next Friday and Saturday and before you know it Mike proposes and the few days and nights spent together each week become every day and every night.

The engagement takes place eight months after we meet, and eight months after that we are married. *Badabing badaboom.*

We rent an old paddle wheel boat for a few hours on our wedding day and have a simple ceremony followed by a champagne brunch on San Diego Bay for eighty guests. It's a gorgeous day and we enjoy sharing our commitment with so many close friends and family as the gentle ocean breeze tousles hats and hair-dos. I finally meet Mike's Vermont family this week and feel so incredibly blessed to have such amazing new people in my life.

Our wedding boat

Mike and I tearing up the dance floor on our special day

9

Our beautiful wedding day on the San Diego Bay

When we look back on this day now we recognize that in large part most of the people on this ship for our special day are friends and family that have remained in our lives. It shows us the depth of our relationship with one another and others, and that's a really great accomplishment and feeling.

The week after we are married we leave for a ten-day European honeymoon and tour France, Germany and Italy. We ride a wave of bliss and innocence, taking in sights and experiencing different cultures and food. It's exhilarating to both of us. We have a shared commonality, the love of travel and exploration.

We return from Europe to a condominium we have rented in La Jolla, just steps from Windansea—a well-known surf beach. It is a nice sized apartment with a peek-a-boo view of the ocean facing a parking area and another condo unit. We like it and blend our belongings together. Neither of us has accumulated much in the way of possessions so we fill the walls and shelves with our stuff and add a few beach-themed doodads and various framed posters that we find during our summer travels to various San Diego art and street fairs.

Our condo has everything we need. Lots of light, a large kitchen and family room, two bedrooms, two bathrooms, and a balcony that runs the length of the unit. We have a few plants and of course I bring Rally and Mahalo along, but other than those living creatures, we don't have to be too mindful of anything else but our jobs and having fun when we are not working.

In the fall of 1994, after our wedding, we host a bow tie and mini-skirt party at our condo and invite forty friends to what amounts to a crazy booze fest with most of us scantily clad. I make vodka-laden Jell-O shooters and we top the concoctions with whipped cream from a can. The party is an eclectic assembly of folks we have both amassed in our separate lives and now commingled to include every color and orientation of the rainbow. The B-52's play on the stereo, the laugher crescendos and we go through over a hundred shooter cups and a lot of whipped cream. Our friends still talk about this party; it was a memory-maker to be sure.

Mike and I eventually settle into a routine of sorts and create some marital rituals. Weekdays usually consist of a morning run or walk for me, and high-energy aerobic dancing classes in the afternoons, while Mike remains committed to attending karate classes a few evenings a week. We try to have dinner together every night, but Mike is still working at Taco Bell and often doesn't get home until very late. On the nights we do manage to have dinner, it is often just simple fare, or we dine out. On Friday nights we usually opt for the Mexican restaurant that is a mere sixty steps from the front of our condo and like the '70's show, *Shirley and Laverne*, we schlemiel and schlimazel our way over there for tableside guacamole, enchiladas, and especially for their fantastic margaritas. Sunday mornings we eat breakfast at a restaurant that overlooks the cove in La Jolla. We sit, soak up the sun, and enjoy the view while we munch on French toast or eggs with basil and feta and take in vast quantities of hot fragrant coffee.

We love and appreciate our lifestyle. We enjoy the amazing coastal temperatures and I often overhear Mike bragging about the weather to his East Coast family while they share stories of trudging through the snow or enduring incessant humidity. They deal with ice storms while we ride our bicycles along the coast in t-shirts and shorts.

Rehydrating after a bike ride on Coronado Island in San Diego

Living this carefree lifestyle is liberating and we are both so happy because we aren't spending our spare time doing things we do not appreciate or enjoy.

One of the things we like the best about where we live is the proximity to the ocean, replete with incredibly attractive surfer boys and girls; but the urban setting is a huge draw too. We have so many restaurants, markets, shopping and entertainment all within walking distance. Our cars often do not move over the course of a weekend. I work about twenty miles away so I am good at making lists and bundling up errands either on the way to or from my job. Mike is very close to where he works but chooses to drive in case he needs to run any work errands during the day. We usually cycle or walk to go where we need to go on the weekends.

So things are sweet and we feel blessed but this is all about to change. We have no idea at the time just how lucky we really are because if we did, we would have held on tightly to those times and refused to let go.

Two

The Italian War

Not long after we get settled into our condo and are enjoying our lives, a couple of young Italian guys move into the unit below us. The walls are not thick enough to mask the noise they make and we can hear their voices and music well into the night. At first, we let it go, but then it becomes habitual. Mike goes down and introduces himself to these guys and asks if they could make an effort to be quieter. "Sure," they say, being agreeable. We quickly learn that it is not going to happen. Night after night we have techno heart-pumping music pulsating into our bedroom. Apparently these guys are wealthy and do not need to work, so they sleep all day, while we are at work, and then they go out to the night clubs after dark and come back around midnight to continue the party with friends—meaning women—often until two or three in the morning.

We talk to the offsite property manager but nothing changes and there is no resolution. We try earplugs but they do not help. One morning, a month into this, sleep deprived and utterly frustrated, Mike starts dropping ten-pound weights on the floor and then places his stereo speakers downward and blasts his stereo as loud as it will go. They get the message. Within seconds we have two extremely hot-heated guys at our front door screaming at us in Italian. The war begins.

One of the guys meets a blonde-haired American girl and she ends up moving in over time, along with her golden retriever. She keeps the dog crated on the occasions when they are not home—which is often—so a new obnoxious noise surfaces, that of a crying dog. We are beside ourselves. Eventually the woman and her dog leave but the guys carry on.

Three

Home Ownership

The neighbor's ceaseless noise causes Mike and I to start talking about what it would be like if we bought a house. A house with no shared walls so we wouldn't have to put up with the goings-on of others. We both begin to enter a fantasy state creating this marvelous place in our minds where everything will be perfect and we can control our world and choose our neighbors. Mike scans the newspapers for home sales and we start putting money aside. We know we cannot afford anything near the coast so we look about twenty miles inland. In the interim we break our lease on our beach condo and move east to an apartment in Tierrasanta so we can save more money with a cheaper, smaller, and unfortunately darker place.

This new apartment is a trip. The complex is huge and there is high turn over. We have a single parent next door to us who likes to yell at her kids and the kids like to bounce off the shared wall. We bite our tongues. Once Mike banged on the wall to send the message that her kid needs to chill out and she comes over with a baseball bat and clangs it on the ground as a responding message that next time it would be Mike's head instead of the concrete getting thumped.

We are motivated to get out of this tight living space and fast. We lose our patience and with it, our ability to compromise, our fantasy life with a home awaits us so, within a year, and a higher paying job change for each of us, we find a house we both like that is still under construction. The builder is offering an attractive purchase arrangement called a 3-2-1 buy down where the rate will increase from five percent to a fixed seven percent over the span of three years. It is a two-story home in a nice upcoming, and recently undeveloped, area of San Diego County called Scripps Ranch and it is located in a suburban setting. The homes are single-family dwellings but built with so little room between them that you could literally walk between each home with your arms outstretched and nearly touch two separate dwellings at the same time. Much to our chagrin, most of our friends refer to our home as a townhome because they are so closely set together.

Our first home in the state of construction

This will be our future family room

Another thing the builder did was parcel and fence the properties in such a way that the backyard fence line jogs in to the rear right corner of each home so that no one owner is able to walk completely around their own property. The idea is that by doing this each owner gets a bonus yard on one side. Irrespective of the close proximity and townhome feel, we are so excited to have a place of our own. With the home under construction we get to pick out the carpets, wall paint, door styles, lighting fixtures, and doorknobs. Mike tires with the details and by the time it gets to the doorknobs he looks at me, shrugs, and says he does not care, as long as they work.

In December 1995 we move into our new home and we feel like we have arrived.

A good many weekends are spent laying down a lot of cash. We purchase furniture and accessories to fill our 1700 square foot home. We acquire appliances and new, somewhat impersonal things to hang on its walls. Since it is new construction and the backyard is nothing but dirt, we design and contract to have hardscape, irrigation and a palm tree laden landscape installed. Now we are homeowners.

With less disposable money, the gym membership and karate lessons can no longer be financially sustained and instead are replaced with neighborhood walks and after work gardening sessions. I start doing more in home cooking and begin experimenting with more creative and often time consuming recipes, some are hits and some are misses but they are all eaten since dining out is no longer as frequent with the expense of our mortgage and bills.

We continue to of course to prioritize time spent with friends and we do low key entertaining in our home. We are fortunate to meet several terrific couples in the neighborhood that we like to socialize with and when invited to their homes for dinner or drinks it feels like date night.

Mike and I make an effort to get to know all of our immediate neighbors. We don't want to be known as the people to simply enter the house via car through a quickly opening and closing garage door that never interact with anyone else. The family who lives to the left of us is nice enough. They are a couple from Poland with a young son named Alan. They are quiet, cordial and for the most part keep to themselves. We stay on a "hello, how are you?" basis and only share a glass of wine with them during the holidays. She makes an effort to engage while he remains stoic and reserved. On the other side we have the recently divorced and very bitter mother that really should have refrained from procreating. She is a mess. After her husband left her, her father purchases this brand new home as an investment and moves his daughter and her three young kids in. It does not take long for this home to become the neighborhood eyesore. It is not hers, she isn't paying for it and so there is neither care on her part, nor concern to keep it maintained and looking decent. Soon the landscape dies, the garage door comes off its tracks, and both her front and backyard, in addition to her garage and home are littered with debris, trash and weeds.

In a gesture of goodwill, Mike goes over to assist this woman with a broken garbage disposal after she asks for his help. He is aghast when he returns, telling me that the carpet and counters are covered with fast food wrappers, half eaten food, and the contents from boxes of cereal are strewn across the floors. There are even discarded soda cans on the ground in her home. I experience the same thing when I offer to pet sit her poodle, the house is a filthy mess. Wash and clean clearly is not a part of her vocabulary or level of comprehension. We fear for a neighborhood roach infestation.

This woman is so depressed from her divorce that she just stops caring, and unfortunately her children and the neighborhood are paying the price. Her children go door to door to our neighbors asking if they can *borrow* some milk. She becomes our suburban equivalent to the Italian boys nightmare in La Jolla. We are frustrated that a single person can have such an impact on our property value and quality of life. How could this have happened? We chose our home so carefully and we have made significant sacrifices to get here. We have money and our sweat tied up in this home and our possessions. This is not supposed to happen.

We let our emotions get the best of us and send a scathing letter to her parents and the board overseeing the development's covenants, conditions and restrictions (CC and R's). They both get involved and some improvement is made, but the relationship is extremely strained and her backyard remains in a dump yard like state.

Meanwhile our simple palm yard expands as I decide to add more colorful plants and flowers. I don't mind the hand watering as the yard is small so over time the day lilies, exotic grasses, lantana, and various vines that I add in addition to the palms grow up and out. Now I am spending just as much time pruning as I do watering, but the cozy, lush feel is inviting and the native field mice and predatory hawks love it.

A backyard in the making

The yard with the palms is starting to take off

A cozy sitting place in the yard

A few years later, in the fall of 1998, Mike is reading the Sunday newspaper and casually mentions to me how much our property has gone up in value. We start to notice for sale signs pop up on the lawns of neighbors and become interested. The fantasy of the perfect, quiet neighborhood once again becomes the topic of our discussion on walks and during meals. Selling next to a slob will be tricky, but it will mean a better investment with nice, decent neighbors. A few conversations lead to more and then the next thing we know we were traveling even further north and inland to look at remote properties in Fallbrook and Valley Center, both areas located within rural San Diego county.

What if we sell our home here in Scripps Ranch and move to a property with acreage in the country? Wouldn't that be great? We will have more room for a garden, space between homes, quiet, maybe put in a swimming pool and get a dog. Who wants to live in stucco-world anyways? What could be more perfect?

Four

A Slice of Country

So in 1999, after a just month on the market, we luck out and sell our home—because of the lush yard thank you very much—and manage to purchase a much larger brand new 2600 square foot one with four bedrooms and two bathrooms in pastoral Valley Center. The house is gorgeous with an open floor plan, a massive fireplace, plenty of light, and some pre-existing landscaping that the builder has installed. It has several queen palms out front at the street, perimeter shrubs and plants around the house, as well as a very sizable lawn out front, plus a fair amount of red apple ice plant on the banks. The rest of the property is simply native or invasive—sagebrush, jimson weed, mustard weed and dandelions. We actually buy this new baby for less than we sell our existing place, amazing both of us. Our new residence is sixteen miles from the nearest freeway and the community has very few amenities. Valley Center has been primarily used for growing oranges and avocados but the movement has slowly begun for growers to chop up these groves and parcel them out to developers at huge profits for new homes. Our local stores include a two story hay and grain establishment that sells chickens and livestock feed on the first floor and rents videos upstairs; a landscape supply place; a place that sells gravel, dirt and stones; one *very slow* fast food drive through called Snoopy's, several mom-and-pop type restaurants that are mediocre at best, a pizza place that doesn't deliver, a post office, a hairdressers, a dilapidated bingo hall, a farm stand, a very smelly convenience store, and an equally smelly dairy farm usually overrun with more migrating Canadian geese than cows.

Our newly constructed Valley Center home

On move day, I go to work at my regular job while Mike takes the day off to coordinate with the movers. We agree that I will go to our old home once he calls me to let me know the movers are finished and I will do the final detail cleaning, get our two cats, pick up some dinner, and then head to our new digs. I get the call and head over. I crate the kitties and put them in the garage and then vacuum, clean all the glass, detail the appliances and finish by mopping my way out the door. I wring out the mop as I make my way to the garage, dump out the water, and toss everything in my car. I think about the hard work we put into this place over the last three and a half years and about the good times despite the nasty neighbor lady. But, when the garage door closes and the cats and I drive away, I'll admit, I never even glanced in my review mirror.

Forty minutes later I drive up the pitch-black road in the country towards our new home and see the porch lights illuminated as the cats and I make our way down the driveway. Mike has done so much work just in a single day. Plants line the entry to the house; furniture is in place albeit sparsely laid out since this home is so much larger, but even still, I instantly feel like I have arrived home. Mike has found our kitchen dishes and has them laid out for our dinner. As we munch our meal of simple deli sandwiches in our brand new kitchen we both cannot help but smile as we enjoy the quiet and solitude.

Five

Know Your Neighbors

Within a week of our move Mike meets the inhabitants of the only other house on the street. They are a Mexican family with three children. We had actually already met their youngest son Eddie, or rather saw him on our first few visits to our house before it was officially ours. A young, stocky kid of about eight with a mass of short brown hair, Eddie would be riding his bike around and around the home above ours watching us with curiosity and intent each time we set foot on the property below his. We felt certain that he would be telling his parents about the people he saw coming and going from the home below. Sure enough, the first weekend of our move, while I am at an opera downtown San Diego with my father, Jesus and Lucia and their three kids come to our front door and introduce themselves. They bring us a fresh pie and a warm welcome. Over time we become good friends, both of them always willing to have a nice chat when they see us. Jesus, short and stocky, had watched his house being built as he made his rounds as a garbage collector in Valley Center, and he supplemented his income with side jobs to help buy it. He is generous to a fault, a good friend with a giggling laugh and child-like demeanor. His wife Lucia is petite, sweet and equally as generous.

In the first year our street of two homes reaches its maximum build out with a total of four homes, spaced out over twelve acres of land. At the home directly below us on our sloping street is a couple, Stan and Cindy that has just returned from living in Australia with their two young daughters. They are a delightful and friendly family. Next to them, the home at the bottom of the street is an older retired couple, Paula and Greg, she still very vibrant, flamboyant and politically active, he sadly a shadow of his former self, unable to speak and shaky on his own two feet—a victim of stroke and Alzheimer's.

They say you can't pick your neighbors and although we are all very different, we would not want any others. Over time our neighborhood became like a family. We share cocktails and meals, secrets and ideas, flower bulbs and baked goods, and our time with one another.

Several months after we move in another neighbor living a few streets away calls and tells us that she has found two tiny female puppies that appear to have been abandoned or lost. She says they have been running loose on the country road and out of concern scoops them up and brings them home so they will not be run over or hurt by cars, coyotes or loose dogs. She puts up signs and runs a newspaper notice in hopes of finding the rightful owners—they were clearly dumped and nobody claims them. Already having two dogs of her own, and unable to keep them herself, she insists that they be adopted as a pair. Thus despite really only intending to get one dog *in the future*, Wilma and Betty, two small chow-chow shepherd mix pups come to be ours.

At roughly ten weeks old, and no more than ten pounds each, these two brown and black puppies are writhing bundles of cuteness and energy. We bring them home and after hours of play, we opt to keep them in the garage at night so that the coyotes will not eat them. To provide them with adequate outdoor daytime space, Mike immediately puts up a temporary four-foot fence topped with barbed wire as a further deterrent for roaming coyotes. We decide to put the fence up close to the house so that the access to them is in and out is through the garage, plus a crude gate near the side of the house where the utility boxes are located. There really is no hardscaping behind the house except a few door pads that are no larger than four foot by four foot so the ground of their pen is simply dirt and minuscule pebbles. Mike is both exhausted and feeling accomplished when he finishes the pen. He is covered in scrapes from the barbed wire and bruises but the budget beer he has taken to drinking now—in lieu of our La Jolla days more expensive microbrews—still goes down pretty smooth. The dogs are now safely tucked in behind a metal casing and we hold steady vigilance each evening to make sure that nothing harms them.

Betty and Wilma as puppies

Mike finishing the first of many dog enclosures

Within the first week the puppies are introduced to Rally and Mahalo. The cats are not sure what to make of these tiny beings and the puppies, intrigued and boisterous, both get a little paw bat on the nose when they come too close to each cat. The pups decide that the cats are the indoor bosses and they are going to steer clear of them. They are not yet potty trained, and we do not intend to keep the dogs in the house, so the interactions will be minimal and supervised, but at least we set the stage so the dogs will never terrorize the cats. While Rally and Mahalo remain safely indoors, Betty and Wilma begin to rule our evenings and weekends. They are just so adorable, fun, and entertaining. The neighbor kids feel the same way and it is not uncommon for us to come home from work and find kids cutting a path through our backyard to visit the puppies or, lingering nearby waiting for an invitation to join us in puppy games. We take the girls out of their dusty pen in the evening when we get home from work and let them run around on the lawn. They race back and forth, and then do play attacks, rolling around, barking and yelping. Eventually the neighbor kids on both sides of us get puppies of their own and the visits cease.

I come home one day and notice that the phone is not working. Betty and Wilma have recently taken up the art of digging and decide to dig near the side of the house where the utility lines lay. They dig deep enough to find the phone line and sever it. I take the next day off from work to wait for the phone guy to come out and repair the line at our expense of course. We do not want a repeat of this so Mike changes the configuration of this temporary enclosure to remove access to the phone line. He sustains more scratches and scrapes, says a few choice words under his breath, and another cheap domestic beer is consumed.

Eventually wanting to give the dogs more room to roam we decide we will fence close to an acre and a half of our nearly three acre property. I think we would have decided to do this anyways, but having these two new growing outdoor beasts accelerates the need. Jesus, being the handyman, is game to go in on half of the cost for one side of the fence that will separate our two properties. Mike convinces Jesus to go with upgraded black vinyl-coated chain link instead of the standard unfinished silver. Jesus acquires and brings home all the materials and proceeds to show Mike how to build a fence. It is July when they start and hotter than Hades. Jesus works the way he did in

Mexico twenty years ago, which means manually, and is undeterred by the heat. His two young sons help too and with post diggers and a bucket of water to soak the earth, they proceed to pour and dig, and pour and dig some more. We go through a lot of fruit popsicles over the month keeping these guys cool and refreshed.

The fence installation team; Mike is the gringo on the far left

The work to dig the holes for the posts stretches out over several weekends but eventually they are able to create deep cavities in the hard-packed earth for the posts. They fire up the pint-sized cement mixer and haul the bags of rocky sand and water to get the mixture into a wet, pourable state. Then they lug the concoction to each hole and set each one in concrete. They unroll the fence material, stretch it by hand and secured the vinyl fencing to each post. Mike's hands and arms ache at the end of each day but when he is done he is very proud of what he has accomplished. Jesus says he has never seen a white guy work so hard. To this Mike smiles and drinks another beer.

Mike's friend Randy, whose wife found Betty and Wilma, works for a large equipment company and he is able to deliver a sizable skip-loader Mike has rented for us to use over the weekend. I want Mike to cut a swath down the back ravine of our hilly property. Our land is essentially shaped like a "V" in the back and used to harbor a small creek, until someone upstream dammed the water and the thing dried up. Regardless of the creek dam, there is still a water table and the gully is dense with vegetation. The incline is steeper than either of us realizes and Mike nearly flips the skip-loader down the bank of the "V." We decide a swath is not *that* important and that it is probably wiser and safer to just even and smooth the earth closer to the house out a bit before we put in our landscape. Even this proves to be sufficiently challenging so Randy comes over and does much of the job for us gratis. He refuses any payment so we thank he and his wife for their generosity by preparing an elaborate meal replete with wine and spirits, the first of many, many meals we will put on for friends and family at our Valley Center home.

"Cut me a swath Mike"

It is within the first six months of owning our country home that Mike and I finally get take a another *real* trip besides our venture to Europe for our honeymoon five years prior. Home ownership has relegated our vacations to staycations— meaning stay home and do projects—a local long weekend getaway to somewhere close like Catalina Island, or family visits to Montana and Vermont. Now with a recent job move that pays me more, and Mike's income ticking up, we manage to save for a weeklong cruise to Alaska. Tami, the neighbor who gave us Betty and Wilma agrees to take the girls while we are gone, while Jesus' oldest son Benjamin will watch and tend to our cats. Jesus agrees to do a contract job for us and lay down 2500 square feet of cement and drainage in the backyard, turning our dog run from a pile of dirt into a paved run and eliminating the dust we get every time the wind blows.

While we are gone Jesus puts in extensive drainage down the back yard that later we will make into dry riverbeds by covering the areas with large stones and then plant drought tolerant plants nearby to make sure the earth is held in and does not erode. In addition to the cemented section we want for the existing dog area, he also puts in a huge semi-circular concrete pad off the master, family and kitchen areas and scores the areas in large sections. He asks us if we intend to put in a patio cover and we agree so he puts in several brackets that could be used for a wooden patio cover. The brackets stick up all over the place so Jesus puts squares of wood in them so no one slices their knees by running in to the rough edges. It looks very ghetto but it seemed like a good idea at the time.

Jesus and amigos lay our cement patio

Wilma and Betty on fresh cement in their dog pad

28

Our time in Alaska is amazing. We visit many cities and towns including Anchorage, Skagway, and Juneau, and we take in glaciers, whales, wolves, spawning salmon and the beautifully huge mountain of Denali. We come back from Alaska feeling refreshed and with a sense of accomplishment.

We see the dusty earth behind our home starting to look a bit more hospitable but we both know the minimal hardscape we put in is a minor dent in the work we have laid out in front of us. I am excited to get started with designing and installing an elaborate, drought tolerant yard. We have much to do and pay for. With a plan to just take it step by step, we endeavor to keep balance while progressing forward.

Six

"I can't wait to go back to work to rest."

I am anxious to put in a garden of succulents, cactus, fruit trees and grape vines. I start to live, eat and breathe garden shops and catalogs. I look at every plant each house in the area has and I become quite familiar with what I like and do not like. I learn plant names, when they flower, how much water they need, and details on whether the plants can take the extreme summer heat or the colder winter temperatures. Since Mike allowed me to design our first home's garden, he is leaving this one in my hands too. He says, "you did such a great job in Scripps Ranch, I have no doubt you will do a beautiful job here too." Plus, I think it sounds like work to him so he is happy to acquiesce.

I am planning and imagining, but first we need to tackle the existing weeds and vegetation, bring in some planting soil and gravel to prep the area, determine what kind of irrigation we need, and finish the fencing. We have a lot to do.

For weeks and weeks we spend our Saturdays and Sundays, and many times our evenings pulling out weeds and removing sagebrush. Hoes, rakes and shovels in hand, we dig and remove much of the existing shrubs, leaving about ten or fifteen sage bushes in place since they will tie in nicely with the southwest garden I am planning.

Mike shows off his weed-whacking skills

Fortunately Valley Center has a green waste-recycling program so we buy and label five large trash bins for discarded vegetation. Each week we drag the heavy cans down our driveway to the street on pick-up day. Then we drag them back for the next round of weeds and greens to be loaded for the following week.

Before we put in the plants we want the fence complete. Mike approaches our neighbors Stan and Cindy below who have put in a small horse pen for their daughter's pony named Popeye but they are not prepared to do any fencing just yet. So, Mike walks the property line with Stan just to make sure he is in agreement with the placement of the fence between our two properties. We bid out the project and hire a contractor to complete the other three sides, including a ten-foot metal gate at the rear of the property to access the additional acre of our land located in the impenetrable craggy "V" area.

The fencing company charges us $8.00 a foot and with over an acre of property to fence, it is not going to be cheap, but it will certainly get done and that is what is important. Using a gas-powered auger, the holes for the fence posts are dug and the poles are set within the first day. Mike is amazed and kicks himself for not having known about the auger for the first side of the fence he did with Jesus. "For sixty bucks," he says, "I could have saved my back and two weekends worth of digging." Live and learn.

A few days after the cement is cured for the posts, the fence team returns and quickly completes the job. It is wonderful to take off for work early and return to see so much progress. The place is taking shape.

We find another local contractor to make a front electronic gate for us. The lead project manager is a crusty old guy named Frosty who chain-smokes and talks with a thick raspy voice. We pick out light fixtures and explain how we want the pilasters that would frame and hold the gate shaped. We go with a black metal gate cut with the letters "L" and "M" for "Lori and "Mike", though later Mike would claim the letters represent "Lunatic" and "Maniac" for our dogs, or maybe he meant us?

We select a solar charged gate in lieu of electric, but even still Frosty says they'll have to run a trench along the driveway in order to hook-up to the electric for the lights going on top of the pilasters. We also opt for a pedestrian gate. Even though our home is rural and somewhat remote, we want to be able to take the dogs for a walk via a small-keyed gate, versus our fifteen-foot, large, solar-battery gate.

With the gate on order, Mike determines that we need to level out the slope at the front of the house near where one of the front pilasters will be placed to discourage any erosion. Expenses are mounting but Mike is able to get a good price on curved interlocking blocks from a work contact, and has found some free fill dirt available in the newspaper. For several nights in a row, Mike picks up materials at the end of his workday, and then we unload the dirt and bricks when he returns home, building a small retaining wall as we go. It is especially challenging for Mike since he has left the fast food restaurant industry several years ago and is now selling, delivering, and *hauling* linens, uniforms and rugs for a large uniform company. His work is very heavy—and Mike is not a big guy—and his day normally starts between 3:30 and 4:00 am and does not end until 6:00 pm with the commute. He would often tell me, "I can't wait to go back to work to rest," the chores and improvements we are doing being so physically demanding.

When the retaining wall is complete I go and buy a variety of color annuals and small shrubs to fill the top of it so that you will see a splash of color from the road as you approach our entry. There is no irrigation for this new wall so I have to hand water the plants daily to keep them alive and get them established. I under estimate how high the top of the wall actually is and you can barely see the plants peeking over the top of the new wall, but I am determined to help them survive. I go out one evening to give them a drink and many of the plants are gone—either sucked underground by pocket gophers, or eaten from above by hungry rabbits. All that remains are holes and scrappy looking stalks of what had been there. Both critters have apparently decided that we had some pretty tasty eats as I begin to see more and more holes burrowed in the grass and lots of rabbit poop all over the property—the dogs think the poop is a special doggy treat. I respect nature, and these critters were here first, but I can see this becoming an expensive proposition. Soon enough we will be able to leave the dogs out in the larger fenced area to scare the rabbits and other critters off, but until that happens I do some investigating and find that there are special sprays that you can use that *should* act as a deterrent. They have a putrid and revolting smell but they do not phase or deter the wild ones. I buy more plants, and they too get nibbled and then the free fill dirt begins to sprout crab grass that only adds to the maintenance of the wall project. It's too bad the crab grass is so unattractive as the animals are not interested in it at all and it flourishes.

Then I find a retailer online who offers a non-lethal device designed to get rid of gophers for $70. It is an electric plug-in cylinder that emits a sound they are guaranteed not like. I buy it and when it arrives I put the cylinder in the hole and plug it in the first morning after I receive it. When I get home that afternoon it is already broken. The gopher dislikes the sound so much he fills the entire cylinder with dirt and jams the sound box. I mail it back for an exchange and this time the gopher bites the electric cord in half to silence the nerve-wracking sound. I get my money back. I am befuddled so I resort to lethal control, though I like to think now that the gophers still outwitted me. We buy gopher bombs and put them in the gopher's tunnel and then light the end. The idea is a noxious fatal fume goes into their hole and asphyxiates them. I shutter at the thought now, but I was desperate. Fortunately, their holes is so long that they could run to another end and outrun the smoke plume or the bomb would snuff itself out when I buried it so this did not succeed either.

I still laugh when I think about all the bird feeders I put on the property over time. I would often see movement below the bird feeder and a gopher head popping up and quickly back down, stealing seed and then bringing the cache back down into his burrows. They were hungry and I was giving them the horn of plenty. No wonder they moved in closer and doubled in numbers. It was hysterical to catch the dogs watching them too—wanting so badly to get them while safely locked behind the fence of their original dog area.

The pilasters for the gates are poured and the lights are now up and working. It looks so cool to see them lit up at night. We are excited when we get the call from Frosty. He has our gate at last and is ready to do the installation. We are less than thrilled that the gate has to be a swing gate versus a sliding gate, which is a much better gate in terms of durability, but due to the slope and shape of our entry, a slider just is not feasible.

The gate looks great and we feel so proud pressing the remote button to activate the gate when we arrive home from work or when guests visit. It has that "wow" factor to be sure.

The "Lori and Mike" or "Lunatic and Maniac" gate?

Now at last the property is secure for our dogs and it is time to give them more freedom. We start with baby steps at first just letting them access the entire property on weekends and evenings when we are there. But soon enough they will have the run of the place all day long—freedom to chase birds, dig for gophers, chase the mailman's truck while safely secure behind the fence, play, sleep, and get into *a lot* of mischief.

Seven

Dogs, dogs, dogs…

"I think we must have had a mountain lion on the property," Mike tells me one day. "Look at Betty and Wilma, they are covered with spit and bites, like they were mauled or something."

We are horrified and take them to our veterinarian. The vet takes one look at them and gives us a smirking laugh.

"It was no mountain lion," he says, "your dogs have been fighting."

We cannot believe what we just heard, "Our two sweet dogs? Fighting? With one another?" It just cannot be.

The vet tells us this is typical of two type A female littermates. He tells us he has the same situation with father and son Rottweilers he has in his family. He even had to build a fence down the middle of his property to separate them. He wishes us luck, gives us some ointment to put on their wounds, and sends us home.

And then we witness it ourselves.

Mike goes out to feed them very early one morning and something triggers Betty and she attacks Wilma. Within a minute they are in a full-out brawl with one another. Snapping, biting, fighting. Mike runs up to the house screaming for me to come out to help him. It's 5am, and I am fast asleep, startled and incoherent—I jump out of bed and run outside. He is trying to stop them and is attempting to wedge a plastic chair in between them to get them to stop. He goes so far to smack them with the chair but they are oblivious. Betty wants to kill Wilma. I try to intervene, something I later learn is extremely stupid, and find myself with several excruciating puncture wounds on my hands as I try to separate their jaws from one another. And then, as abruptly as it begins, it ends. They both sit side-by-side licking their wounds as if nothing ever happened.

Their wounds are identical to those of the supposed mountain lion. We are in shock. What do we do now?

We do not want to, but we figure our best bet is to find one of them a new home. Since we witnessed Betty instigate the last fight we decide Wilma would be the more adoptable of the two. It's an agonizing decision, but what can we do? We make an appointment with the closest animal shelter for the following weekend and take her in for an evaluation. We surmise this will be a slam-dunk end to our dog problem as Wilma is very sweet and friendly.

We are asked to remove ourselves while two young women access Wilma's personality. They take her into a portable building that has high windows and each woman has a container of dried kibble. The idea is that one of them will shake the kibble while calling Wilma and she will go to that person and get a treat, and then the other woman will do the same. I presume from there they will evaluate her manners, get her to sit, stay and so forth. The women no sooner get Wilma in the room alone when she tries in earnest to jump up and out of the trailer's windows. She is not going to participate in their evaluation, and she is beside herself at being separated from Mike and I. Wilma no sooner goes in that room, and she is coming right back out.

"Your dog has *serious* separation anxiety issues," one of the young women tells us. "She isn't a candidate for adoption."

"Whaaaat?" we say in unison.

We feel defeated, upset and utterly confused. Now what?

On our way back to Mike's truck we meet a nice couple that are walking up to the shelter to look for a companion dog for one they already have. Mike almost has the wife convinced to take Wilma but the guy hesitates and Wilma goes back home with us.

A week later we are at the local farm supply store loading up on miscellaneous garden supplies, a soaker hose for the front retaining wall area, and birdseed for the gophers (ha-ha). Outside of the front door of the business someone has placed the last of the litter of unadopted puppies from an Australian shepherd and chocolate Labrador romance into an apple barrel. One small male and one small female remain from the unintended litter of five.

"What if we got a male dog to break up the dynamics?" I say more as a statement than a question to Mike.

I hold up an adorable tailless brown bundle of joy with pale green eyes and shove him into Mike's face.

"I don't know," he says. But the hesitation is short lived and fifteen minutes later we are on our way back home with a twenty-pound bag of puppy chow and a new puppy to boot.

My little man Pancho

Pancho admires Wilma; they'll be lifelong pals

We name the new puppy Pancho and we introduce him under close supervision to Betty and Wilma. Betty is not super interested but Wilma is and she keeps kneeling and barking at him and then jabbing him with her nose.

The first night we check up on tiny Pancho a dozen times to make sure he is okay with the girls. The next day we play with him on the front grass and then introduce him to the cats. Like Betty and Wilma, he wants nothing to do with the felines; they are way too scary he decides. This is going to be great we think.

Monday comes and it is back to work. It is August of 2000 and very warm so we cannot leave Pancho in the garage, we are going to need to leave him in the smaller temporary pen we still have with Betty and Wilma. We would leave them all out in the larger fenced yard but we are not at that stage yet with the girls, and plus Pancho is so small he could easily fit between the bars of the front gate and that is not safe for him.

Of course, any time you get a new puppy it is all you can think about. All of our coworkers had heard about our dog fighting saga and when we share we have gotten a new puppy to introduce a male into our female doggy duo we are both told that we will probably arrive home to find out that the girls have killed him out of jealousy. Mike phones me to share this and we both endure the workday with ominous pits in our stomachs. I can't recall which of us arrives home first that day but there is profound relief to find we still have three intact dogs and that Pancho is fine and happy.

The fighting subsides and Pancho grows quickly.

*****

I am ready at last to place our first large order for plants and so I order 20 yards of rich planting soil and 10 yards of topper gravel in preparation for the cactus garden. We think we can spread the dirt and gravel by hand but when the truck arrives and drops the load the mounds are enormous—what city person really knows what a yard of soil means? Mike comes to the rescue and makes arrangements to rent a skip-loader for a second time to spread the dirt. The dogs play king of the mountain on the huge pile and bark and chase Mike as he spreads the soil out on the property. It takes two days just to lay the dirt. Back to our respective jobs on Monday, we are thinking about the many, many more weekends ahead of us that will be dedicated to digging, planting and installing irrigation.

Mike moves the dirt pile

Now with the property smooth, the fence, gate and pilasters up, some additional hardscape and drainage installed, we decide we should do one more thing before we start the dense interior planting. We hire a landscaper to install irrigation with spray units along the back sides of the yard and rear fence line. We want the spray to hit both in and outside of the rear fence, as we are still concerned about erosion. Since there is nothing to hold in the earth when it rains, we know we need to secure the earth at our fence line and beyond so it will not create a problem in the future. Once the irrigation is installed, tested and operational, we hire a hydroscaper to lay down $300 worth of wild flower seeds and accompanying fertilizer. Much like highway seed plantings, our backyard perimeter glows a strange bright green until the seeds germinate, grow, spread, and then eventually bloom. Within two weeks we have a profusion of amazing colors and it looks really great.

At long last I place my first order for plants. I spend well over $3000 on the first order, and will eventually calculate that I spend $10,000 by the time all the planting is complete. I order fruit trees and fruit baring vines consisting of fig, lemon, orange, grapefruit, guava, persimmon, pear, grapes and blackberries. I order drought tolerant shrubs of lavender, both Spanish and French, Pride of Madeira, lantana, blooming proteas, birds of paradise, and bougainvillea. And I order a wide variety of cactus and succulents—agaves, aloes, barrel cactus, night blooming cereus, and red-hot pokers. A huge truck comes the following weekend, and though Mike is excited about the yard, he is not so excited about more weekend work, namely digging holes.

A new crop of succulents arrive to plant

Me planting our cacti and succulents

I decide it would be good to create a division in the yard between where we intend to plant the grape vines and fruit trees, and where the cactus and succulents, topped by gravel will go. Another weekend at the landscape store and we purchase a dozen railroad ties. Picking them up, carrying them down the back slight slope, placing them and then bracing them with earth is backbreaking.

The planting takes several weeks. We purchase really heavy wooden stakes and thick wire to create a trellis for the vines that extend down the lower right side of the property adjacent to the railroad ties. This task means breaking out the pole digger again for Mike, which he is not too thrilled about. In the future we will put more vines in at the bottom of the property because I want to make my own wine and for those we borrow a friend's gas-powered auger making Mike very happy.

In hindsight, we wish we had opted for something other than railroad ties to put next to food-baring trees and vines because the creosote never stops weeping from those old ties. Oh well, another lesson learned.

Next, we need to figure out irrigation for all these new plants. Since we are placing them all over the fenced portion of the acre property we decide to tackle this after we place them in the ground. We hire a landscaper again to install irrigation for all the trees and then Mike and I put in drip irrigation for the grape and blackberry vines. We also put in drip irrigation along the fence for the bougainvilleas as the spray for the hydroseeding is designed to water a five foot strip, and will not do the deep watering needed to get these vines established. We learn an awful lot about irrigation.

By now Pancho is getting bigger and we begin to let the dogs out more during the day when we are gone. No mishaps for the dogs, but some of the sprinkler heads get snapped during dog races to see who can be the first dog up or down the back embankment. The fact that Pancho is part lab also means that he is a water dog and so yippee, he starts the continual chewing of the drip lines and sprinkler heads. We both become routine shoppers at home improvement stores and at the local irrigation supply store bringing in chewed irrigation noodles and severed sprinkler heads each week for replacement.

One weekend when I am at the Opera with my dad, Mike installs landscape lighting along the driveway up to the house. He trenches all the wiring and does an excellent job. The result is fantastic and we are really excited at the look. We set the timer to illuminate the entry during the dusk and dawn hours. It is great to come home on those moonless nights and have a lighted pathway to the house. Pancho likes the lights too and proceeds to dig up every single one of them, severing the electrical line as he goes. How he avoids electrocution is anyone's guess.

Mike proceeds to rewire and reinstall the lights two more times, and Pancho continues his dig and chew antics. We end up getting some cheap solar lights after that. Those are also eaten and destroyed.

There are other chewing casualties: patio furniture and cushions, hoses, hose sprayers, dog dishes and one rainy night when we put all three dogs in the garage, the brake lines on Mike's truck.

Betty and Pancho are enrolled into an obedience class. We decide we will self-train Wilma since it is not feasible to add a second obedience class to our already very busy lives. For six weeks we take the dogs to the behavior workshop on Saturday mornings and run them through the instructor's exercises on a daily basis. Every evening and every weekend for months we work with the dogs. We teach them to walk on a leash, heel, sit, stay, down, and roll over. We spend a tremendous amount of resources on the dogs with spaying and neutering, shots, treats, licensing, toys, collars, leashes and pest control.

These dogs, along with our two cats, are our kids and we love them all despite the constant draw on our wallets.

The yard is looking good and the cactuses and succulents have been planted in addition to all the other shrubs and plants. We opt not to install irrigation for the cactuses since that defeats the xeriscape purpose and we simply hand water them from time to time to get them established.

The hydroscaping has taken hold and we have blooms of orange, red, pink, gold, purple, and yellow. The flowers are lovely, all different shapes and sizes. The gophers and rabbits also like the new flowers and so the lush growth quickly turns to half eaten patches of color. The irrigation suffers too, and takes a beating from the dogs which in turn causes the patches of half eaten colored hydroscaping to turn to a dusty brown—the sprinklers completely missing them by watering in different directions or overshooting the target.

Pancho takes a liking to listening for and hunting gophers. I watch him patiently listen, then dig like mad. One day

I watch him succeed in making contact with the tiny creature, only to yelp when the creature bites him on the nose. It is just a scratch, no vet visit need for this one.

Another time I watch Pancho tossing something up and down in the air as I see him do with his toys. This time it was a living, breathing baby gopher. I rescue it and move the still live animal off the property. I hope it lived.

With gophers come snakes, and with snakes come dog: snake interactions. We hear about many a dog being bit by rattlers and it is not pretty. Since we both work we know that dogs will not have a chance if they are bitten, whether they were in or outside of their dog-run, they are at risk in this rural setting.

One Sunday afternoon I am working in the yard and see our three dogs barking profusely at something on the ground. I know it has to be a snake or another living creature, and sure enough, it is a baby rattler. I yell for Mike who comes out to help and we get the dogs into their pen and then unfortunately Mike kills the snake. I would have rather he moved it so it could do its job somewhere else.

We hear that snakes don't like gravel and they will avoid crawling across it. Mike finds someone who is giving away reddish-colored lava rock in the newspaper so for more than a week he goes there on the way home from work *again* and rakes the gravel with a shovel and loads it into the back of his pick-up truck. This means that after dinner for all those nights we go out and take the gravel out of the pick-up bed and spread it on top of the bank outside the house to act as a snake deterrent.

A guy comes to town via some kind of dog kennel club advertising snake abatement classes for dogs and horses. We are told that for $100 per dog they will be taught to avoid snakes. So, we shell out three big ones and then bring the dogs to the designated place at the designated time on a Saturday morning. The guy has a snake that he has defanged in a bucket. He explains that he will rig our dogs up with a shock collar and lead them to the bucket so the dogs can smell the snake. The minute the dog is interested he will give the dog a bolt of shock and yell "no" to "scare the bejesus out of 'em." The dog will get the negative association between interest in the snake and pain.

Next, he will walk the dog near the bucket this time getting the snake to rattle its tail. Then he will shock the dog a second time, and again yell "no!"

Finally, after he is sure that the dog gets that smelling and hearing a snake is bad news, he will have the owner of the dog stand about a hundred yards out and he will place the snake between the owner and the dog. If the dog looks interested in exploring what the writhing thing is, it gets another shock, now bringing the senses trio to smell, sound and sight.

Lastly, he will ask the owner to call their dog and clap their hands and watch to make sure the dog does a wide loop around the snake, otherwise it will be subjected to another negative shocking sensation.

Wilma goes first and she does pretty well. She is interested in the snake during the first two tests, gets shocked, and gets the message. When it comes to seeing the snake and then being called she trots right over to Mike and is safely returned to our truck without too much fanfare.

Betty is second for our little trio and is more nervous about the situation than interested in the snake. When it comes to running to Mike when she is called she just takes off. She is so scared of all the shocks and high stimulus that she just wants out of there. The guy leading the class is pretty full of himself in an "I am the almighty snake abatement training guru" kind of way and he just looks at us in disgust as we wrestle to catch Betty, return the shock collar to him, and load her also into the truck.

Pancho is third. He is a bigger boy now but a timid dog. When the guy introduces Pancho to the bucket he does not want anything to do with it and turns his head and dives it right into the guy's crotch to hide.

There is another look of disgust on the guy's face, and a look of sheer terror on Pancho's face. The guy does his best to get Pancho to smell and hear the snake. When it comes time for Pancho to see the snake he once again hides his face in between the guy's legs, then he beelines it to me, running a half circle around the snake as he should, and gives me the same crotch head thrust. It is a fast $300 spent and we really hope they will remember what they learned.

Then it happens again—another dogfight. This one is terrible, and we are not even there to witness it. Mike is petting Wilma and notices the bites and bloodstains, but this time her teeth are also damaged. Her breath is absolutely hideous and the roof on one side of her mouth is hanging down. It is a Sunday morning and our regular veterinarian is not available so we are obliged to go to an expensive emergency animal clinic for help. We drive there with Wilma and wait to be seen. The vet on call says this injury is way beyond her ability to correct and refers us to a doggy dentist located in the city, 40 minutes away. The doggy dentist is from Beverly—cha-ching—Hills and after hanging around there for an hour comes out and tells us he can *certainly* help us and for us to leave Wilma and come back in about five hours for her. He will put a temporary plate in the top of her mouth and then rewire her two canines so they can be stabilized to re-root themselves and not be lost. He tells us to plan on this costing around $3800. "Okay," we say and then we get in the car dazed and opt to go back home and wait out the five hours. We are at home and prior to leaving we feed Betty and Pancho and the two cats and notice that Betty also has putrid breath. Sure enough, she too has damaged teeth and infected gums. We call the Beverly Hill's vet and he is more than willing to do the second surgery for us. So we haul Betty back to the city and hang out. We end up going to Coco's for dinner and then just sit and read magazines until after midnight. The Beverly Hill's vet tells us that since this injury is all as a result of a dogfight that we will need to get a cone for Betty's head and he doesn't have one. So, with groggily dogs released and in tow, we head back to the emergency animal clinic who is still open to buy a cone for Betty at what is now one o'clock in the morning on Monday. All said and done, with the emergency vet visit, the two surgeries, and the medications we have spent a shit-load of money on doggy dentistry.

After the wounds heal we decide to seek professional help and hire a dog psychologist we have heard about that guarantees he can get our dogs to end these aggressive antics. It costs $100 per one-hour visit. He comes in his special K-9 van, bringing his own German shepherd along. The dog exhibits the epitome of restraint and obedience. He is huge and perfectly mindful of all his owner's commands. The psychologist places a shock collar on each of our dogs and then walks him or her through a series of exercises. He focuses mainly on Betty, as she is our problem child. He explains how we need to establish control and a hierarchy by treating Wilma extra special to the point of ignoring Betty. Feed Wilma first, Wilma gets treats first; Wilma goes out the gate first when we walk them, etc. This is to establish who is the next in line after her alpha human companions, Mike being numero uno and me being dos. He also suggests that we buy a muzzle for Betty so that she cannot attack Wilma. It is his opinion that Betty can be reformed. We are optimistically hopeful and relieved. Betty is mindful in his presence and we try really hard to follow his instructions and examples after he leaves. He visits us five times and then we decide to take it from there.

Our girls, Betty and Wilma

Eight

An Eye Full

It's fall of 2000 now and I have ordered and received around five cubic yards of grapefruit and cantaloupe-sized rocks the color of quail's eggs to create our dry riverbed. The pile is massive. I over-ordered, again. It must be a spatial thing. I use our *new* wheelbarrow to move them down the back of the property, since the old one was destroyed when Mike tried to launch a 200 pound boulder into it and it flattened the entire thing into a shape like a scrapped Chevy with a broken wheel. At least the new wheelbarrow we got for *free*—we bought so many supplies at the home improvement store that they forgot to add the thing to our tab when we wheeled up so many items to the check out stand inside of it.

I move my equally distributed rock piles with gloved hands slowly down the side of the hill, placing each stone precisely where I want it creating a bed several rocks deep. The bed itself will be meandering in width and shape to match the contour of the hill. I'm going for an authentic look here and my shoulders are killing me. Jesus waves to me nightly as he sees me spending a good hour or two each evening carrying and placing rocks. Sometimes I am not sure what he thinks when he sees me working like a man all the time. Mike is not really helping me with this project, he is in need of non-physical time—while for me it feels good, sort of, because I sit at a desk all day long.

It takes me a good solid week to get the riverbed complete and I still have lots of rocks left over. I decide to create some *official* walking trails that go down through our fruit trees and grape vines, and then swing around to come up different directions through the desert fauna we've planted. The work takes me another week since I'm having to wheelbarrow large loads of rocks across the gravelly surface to get them to the other side of the yard. Of course I get easily distracted too and find myself pulling the stray weed in between moving all the rocks just for the distraction. My lower back spasms and I keep feeling lightheaded from all the stooping but I ignore it and keep working on creating my walking path borders.

On my way to work one day I notice a vacant lot that is for sale and it occurs to me that whoever buys this lot and builds another office complex on it is simply going to kill all the wonderful gazanias that are blooming all over it. Maybe we could dig some of these up and transplant them to our own yard. Surely they'd survive since they are not being watered by anyone right now and they look spectacular. There is a number on the sell sign and I call it. I get the agent and ask if I can dig up some of the plants growing on the lot. The guy acts like I am a complete idiot and say "sure lady" like it is the oddest request in the world. I tell Mike I want to go over there on Saturday with his truck and he agrees to come with me. Mike had bought me one of those day-glow orange vests like the highway workers wear to use when I walk the dogs at night and he insists that we both wear them when we dig up the plants so that we look *official*. I feel like a complete dork, hoping no coworkers happen to drive by on their way to the office this Saturday while I'm out here removing plants from a vacant field.

We completely fill the back of Mike's truck up with plants and then bring them home. After lunch Mike starts by planting some on the property perimeter where the hydroseeding has died, and I take to planting them near the dry riverbed, and a few here and there where all our cactuses are planted. We wedge our shovels into the gravelly hard dirt and stick the roots into each off center slice of a hole and step on the earth to make sure the plants don't slip back out. We are unable to get through the entire load in one day and the task carries on for a few days, followed by hand watering or sprinklers in case of the perimeter plants. We're excited to be getting free landscaping so we repeat the process the following weekend. We get a ton of these South African beauties in brilliant shades of yellow and orange stripes planted and they look really nice. Over the course of the next several months they multiply and look brilliant.

If this photo were in color you would see the plethora of color

Of rocks and cacti

It's December now and the holidays are upon us. Two of my close girlfriends at the time convince me to put up a holiday tree so I do. I host a ladies tea party replete with cucumber and cream cheese sandwiches, homemade scones and earl gray tea. We're relaxing and talking and I notice this sensation in my right eye of looking through mercury. It is unsettling and I am not sure what it is. I dismiss it but then notice it continues for several days. I call my eye doctor and share what is going on and they tell me to come in immediately, it could be serious. I have had a lot of eye surgeries over the years in this eye for various reasons so they are concerned. I arrive and my eye doctor takes a peek and say, "I need to get a retinal specialist in here for this one Lori." Another doctor comes in and confirms that I have a detached retina, meaning my eyeball is torn and the fluid that is supposed to be hanging out in the back is seeping through, hence the dark mercury halo I am seeing. The doctor proceeds to tell me that I am going in for surgery pronto—as in immediately this afternoon. He says these things are brought on when an eye is stressed and if someone is lifting too much. Opps!

The surgery goes well, followed by a second one because it reoccurs. My doctor stresses that I am not to be moving wheelbarrows of heavy stones and avoid any jarring movements. At least the bulk of the heavy stuff is behind me so this is good news as far as I am concerned. Disappointingly the surgery has us cancel a large holiday party we'd planned for New Year's Eve with all our neighbors—what can you do?

Nine

The vase, the muzzle, and you go this way and I'll go that way

Apparently I am not the only one with a medical issue.

Mike tells me Wilma is not eating one morning. He says she is acting *funny*. I go outside and Wilma is making a terrible noise that sounds like screaming. She is beside herself. I gently place my hand on her back and she cries in agony. We can't figure out what is wrong with her, there is no blood, no injury. Mike leaves for work and I call into the office to let them know I will be late. The vet office opens in an hour and I keep checking on Wilma. She is now sitting by herself at the front of the property near the swing gate and she is shaking. I'm worried because this would be a primo opportunity for a violent attack from Betty; we've learned that she will look for the moments of weakness and seize the opportunity. I put Betty in the smaller dog pen with Pancho to eliminate potential conflicts. At 8:00am I call the vet and tell them I am coming. I manage to get a very distressed Wilma into my car and get her to the vet. They tell me they will call me once they know what is going on. They sedate her and take x-rays. A sliver of bone has managed to lodge itself crossways inside her colon, slicing its way down as it went. The vet rubber gloves it and gently removes the lacerating offender, much to Wilma's and my relief.

While Wilma is finishing up her round if antibiotics to stave off any internal infections, I happen to notice Betty is licking herself, down there, a lot. There is actually even some white puss that indicates we've got a problem Houston. I make an appointment with a different vet while ours is on vacation, and this time come home early from work to get her into an afternoon appointment. The woman veterinarian and I manage to wrestle sixty pounds of chow-chow on the examining table and flip her on her back so she can see what is going on.

"She has an inverted vulva, that is the source of this problem."

"What?" I ask, having no idea what she is talking about.

"Her business is tilted, so basically when see urinates she is peeing on herself and it isn't getting the chance to dry out."

What we are seeing is a yeasty mess Betty is carting around between her legs.

"We could do surgery for this, or you can try treating just with some antibacterial ointment."

Having just dropped a hefty amount recently for doggy dentistry and Wilma's surgery, I opt for the topical treatment and buy the drugs and leave. Twice a day I now have to get Betty in an upside down position and put some goop on a Q-tip and then on her. She takes it pretty well and we begin to notice more spring in her step after a week of treatment.

In April we take a trip to New Mexico. Having planted our southwest garden of cactus I become intrigued with the décor and the look of the Santa Fe style full of Indian influences and cheery kokopellis. We fly to Albuquerque and then rent a car to visit Santa Fe and Taos. We hire a professional pet sitter, not wanting to risk leaving any dog conflicts in the care of Jesus' son—we would feel terrible if something happened on his watch. We communicate with the sitter what has been going on between Betty and Wilma so she can be sure to feed Wilma first and watch for any signals of aggression. She charges $16 per visit and we have her come twice a day—once in the morning to let the dogs out of their pen and feed them, and then again at night to feed them a second time and put them back in their pen. This means for a seven-day vacation we are paying $224 plus tip. It's the going rate for pet care, I've checked, but it still hurts.

I become enamored with the Santa Fe style and buy many decorative items during our New Mexico trip. I spend thousands of dollars on credit purchasing clay Indian pots from the Acoma tribe, a Taos' drum, beaded moccasins just for display, rugs, kiva ladders, wall hangings, blankets, trivets, etc. I decide right then and there I want to decorate the interior of our place so that it is completely southwest inside and Mike likes the idea too. I'm a woman on a decorating mission despite the costs.

Lots of Santa Fe touches

Peering into our living room

We return home and our pet sitter reports out that there were no problems while we were gone. We are relieved.

*****

I want to put in a much nicer small dog run on the side of the house. The temporary one Mike put up when we first got the dogs looks so impoverished and just has to go.

"We have this backyard that is taking shape and we still have this hillbilly dog fence. It looks terrible." I tell him one day.

We are not intending to put up yet another fence, but when we have guests over we really don't want to have them constantly accosted by our three crazy hounds. Plus, we try leaving the dogs out all night a few times and it is an utter disaster. They bark and carry on the entire time and that is not cool when you have neighbors or value your sleep. So we price wrought iron fencing panels at the home improvement store, measure where we want them to go and buy the appropriate amount.

My credit card is taking a huge beating with all the constant spending and my debt is ballooning. I cast my swollen money woes to the wind and opt to go to the spa today for a massage, facial and pedicure while Mike *manages* the fence install.

We hire Jesus to do the install for us and he does a wonderful job. The fence enclosure this time is much smaller and has both the utility door to our master water closet inside of it, as well as a small window that is set just over our master toilet. We fill the space with gravel so the dogs are not on dirt again and move in their three doghouses. Mike then takes down the old fence and donates the materials to a community outreach program.

Wilma takes to becoming the last one to come when called for "night-night" time once the new pen has been installed. She goes to the end of the orchard and hides while Betty and Pancho obediently come and go into the dog run at night. Mike calls and calls her using his *sweet voice* and she makes her way behind the fig tree and crouches. Mike walks down through the fruit trees and can see Wilma making her way to the other side of the yard above the cactus garden, skulking along the fence line as she goes. Eventually Mike has to resort to grabbing her collar to *assist* her in making her way to her sleeping quarters. Inside the pen there is jostling to see which doghouse Wilma wants. She growls Pancho out of the big Igloo doghouse and makes him sleep in one of the smaller square ones.

Wilma's antics take on the form of a routine. Mike gets Betty and Pancho in the pen and loves on them, then spends the next ten minutes locating, chasing and then loving up Wilma before *assisting* her into the dog enclosure. He rarely gets angry with Wilma figuring if he does it will serve to only insight Betty.

Most days the dog conflicts are minimal, a growl, snarl or bite. Now with Betty's infection under control she is obviously feeling more vigor and she begins to challenge Wilma again. We start leaving Betty in the dog run in the day and let Wilma and Pancho out since they never have conflicts. Timid Pancho just steers clear of Wilma when she is in a *mood*. The muzzle goes on Betty when we get home in the evening and she can come out and interact. She hates the muzzle and fights us on it, but we win and her mouth is secured behind black breathable mesh. She tries a few times to pick a fight with Wilma, nosing Wilma behind the neck but Wilma doesn't take the bait. She holds her ground but doesn't take advantage.

They are an odd lot these dogs, each an unplanned creature in life as far as we can tell. They have a profound impact on our quality of life and how we spend our time, and especially how we spend our money. They are lucky we are so sentimental, caring and committed.

One of most vivid memories we both have when we reflect back to this time is sitting out on our back patio in reclining chairs with our Mexican chiminea fired up, a little music on low, enjoying the moon and stars shining so brightly while our team of dogs lie at our feet, taking off from time to time to chase rabbits or howl at the coyotes passing by. We created such a lovely yard and there were many happy times just relaxing and appreciating all our hard work and the bounty of it all—and then it was back to work again.

I stop by my favorite nursery again on my way home from work one Friday night and load more plants including a dozen rose bushes into my Volkswagen beetle. I had been to San Diego's nearby wine country recently and noticed how they planted rose bushes at the end of many of their grape vines. It added some nice color and contrast to the leafy vines. I think it may have worked as a bug deterrent or pollinator attractor for the grapes, although I'm not certain that this is true. Then I hit the farm stand at the bottom of the grade near our community. I load up on oranges, avocadoes, tortillas and greens. Mike helps me unload everything when I get home and cannot believe how much I can fit into my small car. Saturday morning I go to the egg stand at the end of our main road for a dozen. I make Mike and I a huge breakfast of huevos rancheros and fresh squeezed orange juice. It is perfectly delicious. Sufficiently satiated, Mike and I spend all day planting the rose bushes. Sunday afternoon I go to yet another nursery that is in our community *just to look* and find an adorable metal trellis. I also find a kokopelli weather vane and a number of statues I want to put in the yard that include a snake, a coyote and a fox. I think it will be fun to walk down the paths and happen upon these creatures. They will compliment the "stay on path" sign we had made recently at the San Diego Fair as a joke for our walking paths. I come back home and get Mike to bring me back in his truck. I buy all the doodads and we load up his truck and then proceed to unload and place our new items in our yard. The trellis is going to be amazing but with the high winds in our community it will need to be staked. Mike works on this and gets the thing secured, then he hammers in the base for the weather vane.

Tonight we sit with cocktails on our back patio and admire our hard work. We frequently tell friends that, "when that gate closes on Friday night be often don't leave again until Monday morning," which is a true statement, except to go to the hardware store.

"We should put in a chicken coop and get some hens so we can have our own fresh, humane eggs," I say to Mike as he swigs his beverage.

"I also think it would be cool to get some peacocks."

I can hear Mike exhale, just trying to relax for a few hours before its time for bed and time for the Monday workday.

"Maybe we should get one of those cute pygmy goats to help us with the weeds," I add.

"And it would be fun to rescue a burro and give him a secure home. We could build a pen outside of the back fence on the level area before the ravine. He could make friends with Popeye."

"You're killing me," he simply says as he quaffs his beer. Enough said I guess.

Another work-week starts and I come home to find one of the rose bushes we had just planted plucked from its earthy home and strewn on the front grass, fried by the hot summer sun. "There is twenty dollars wasted in a matter of days," me thinks. I know you can't scold a dog for doing something that happened in the past, there is no relation for what has occurred or what it did so unless you catch it in the act you have to hold your tongue. Nevertheless I hold up the burnt plant and shake it at Pancho. "Did you do this?" I ask him in a menacing tone. I glare at him and he can tell I am upset and he makes himself scarce by running and hiding in his doghouse.

This pulling and playing with plants continues and I find recently procured and carefully planted flora in different spots throughout the property, mostly in unsalvageable states of wilted decay. Once in a while I get lucky and am able to replant the specimen, but Pancho is on to me and proceeds to remove and drag the same plant victim to another locale the following day or week. Fortunately the cacti remain unmolested.

One of my coworkers has recently moved rural like Mike and I and has purchased several llamas—he wants to morph from his corporate job into running llama backpacking tours throughout California's rugged mountains. They are interesting creatures and I take to learning more about them. I discover that we have an alpaca, a close relative of the llama, breeding farm near where we live and I am intrigued. I visit the farm and learn about their amenable dispositions and how weavers pay big bucks for their fur. I tell Mike I would like to look at getting one and we investigate the cost. They're expensive animals, starting around $1200 each. Fortunately my finances put the kibosh on many of my fantasy animal purchases from alpacas to chickens and coop or we would have spent what remaining spare time we already didn't have tending to more mouths and needs. My coworker does however share with me some of his llamas' pooh. Seriously, I learn that llama manure is really rich and terrific for your plants so I purchase a five-gallon pail with a lid and start carting it to work—*free* fertilizer and I am excited. My coworker Dale brings home the pail and fills it with manure that evening and then hauls it back to me the next morning. I pull in my Volkswagon next to his huge dually truck and we make the exchange. I stick the goods next to my car during the day to eliminate my car from smelling like a barnyard and that evening put the stuff in my trunk for the commute home.

The first time I bring home a pail of llama pooh our dogs are thrilled. I am told the stuff quickly dissolves and so with gloved hands I spread the stuff on the hillsides. I probably should work the turds into the earth, versus just flinging them on top, but I am lazy and short on time so I bypass the extra step. The dogs feed on the poop snacks and in the morning there is little left. This goes on for several weeks: the bucket exchange with Dale and then little poop pellets being spread all over our property, and the dogs promptly feasting. A year later I'd still happen on the occasional turd, dried and crunchy and never dissolved.

*****

Valley Center is a beautiful place, and though it seems like we are forever working on our property the quiet respites—every now and then—definitely feed our souls.

One evening while enjoying a meal I notice a neon sign in the distance I have never seen before.

"What is that?" I ask Mike.

"It's a neon sign for a new llama farm," he retorts sarcastically.

It is actually a sign for new casino that has just been built nearby that he has mentioned but I guess I didn't put two and two together.

All of a sudden we go from nice and quiet to having six casinos approved and under construction in the area, all on Indian reservation land. This means home prices and employment both are going up in Valley Center. It also means we might get a few more decent restaurants at the casinos, in addition to some entertainment. The sign reminds us that things don't always stay the same, the progress happens even if you don't want it or aren't prepared for it.

Betty's private parts infection is back again. We go for round two with the ointments. We have also become less than diligent with the muzzle, opting to give her more freedom but still keeping her locked up during the day. There aren't any clashes so we feel like we are making headway and may be seeing the end of the fighting issue.

The dogs have taken a liking to our new cement patio set. We buy it at the San Diego Fair at the same time we pick up our "stay on trail" sign. Mike chooses the immoveable, indestructible set after we watched our neighbor's glass patio table and lightweight plastic chairs become a broken heap at the hands of severe Santa Ana winds. The winds played their set like it was simply blowing leaves off a tree as it shattered the glass and twisted the chairs. Our cement set is green and has an umbrella hole in the center. We keep the umbrella in the garage and bring it out only when in use, carefully returning it to the garage each time we are done to preserve it. We've learned, having the first one snapped in half by the wind.

Wilma likes to stand on top of the table and has claimed it as her own. She stands on it to search for cars as they come up the road and is often seen sleeping on it. She guards it jealously from the other dogs and they seem to understand it is her domain. On the occasions I arrive home from work first I see Wilma looking for Mike's work van, a huge lumbering thing that with her keen ears she likely hears from several miles away. She does a joyous launch off the tabletop and down the side of the yard barking and practically bucking with excitement. Then she races towards the front with Betty and Pancho on her heels. By the time Mike arrives all three dogs are circling with anticipation as he backs the step-van into the driveway. Our arrivals at home always cause the same level of excitement and anticipation. It is a warm and rambunctious reception, although not necessarily always welcome—especially when wearing something nice that you really don't care to have covered in dog paw prints and slobber.

Betty's infection keeps returning after each round of antibiotic ointment. We try an oral antibiotic and get the same results—a bit of reprieve followed by another messy outbreak. We talk to our regular vet and opt to get her a vulva tuck. The vet cuts a small incision and then pulls the skin and makes a stitch so Betty's urine stream will go down onto the ground rather than onto herself. She wears a cone for a week to let things heel and we administer another round of medication. Unfortunately we never opted to purchase pet insurance so all these expenses are out of pocket.

Betty is recovering nicely and we see her spirits soar. She becomes animated and very spunky. She truly is a very sweet dog and we are happy to see her being more playful and engaged, although we know we can't let our guard down and be less than diligent with the hierarchy.

All three dogs love to play fetch and we take turns throwing dog toys in various shapes, sizes and colors for them. Betty seems more interested in getting the items tossed and taking off with them. She does not understand the concept of bringing them back to us. Instead she merrily pounces on the toy, grabs it in her mouth, and then runs away, quickly losing interest and simply abandons the object. Wilma and Pancho on the other hand will return again and again for another throw.

One afternoon Mike and I are playing keep away Frisbee from the dogs. Well actually, we are just playing with one another but we have to be swift and precise as Wilma is itching to sink her teeth into it. I grab it and quickly flip the Frisbee to Mike, Wilma running after the thing like a crazy beast. Mike snags it and flings it back and Wilma goes high, trying to snag it in midair. I catch it and do a 360 turn, aiming to sail it back to Mike but instead I get a good chomp on my tush from Wilma. I decide I have had enough of this game and leave Mike to playing Frisbee with Wilma while I go nurse my bruised behind.

Frisbees and skip-loaders are not the only things the dogs like to chase, they also like to take off after the lawnmower when Mike or I cut the grass, and any vehicles that come up the street, especially Jesus' truck, are all fair game for a chase, fortunately the chasing takes place inside our fence.

Sadly, Wilma is a great hunter. Songbirds, roadrunners, rabbits, mice, lizards, and even bees and other flying insects all fall prey. There were quail on our property when we moved in but they quickly left once we got the dogs. The lizards in particular like the dry riverbed and it is not uncommon to see all three dogs circling and scratching rocks trying to catch these speedy reptiles. Most of the time the other animals win, but there are enough carcasses and body parts found to know that isn't always the case.

It's a three-tailed lizard hunt

One Saturday evening Mike and I go out to dine at the home of some friends. When we return, we hit the part of the road that lies equal in depth to the ravine behind our house. As we make the descent towards the turn to go up our street a huge white owl hovers just inside the beam of our Volkswagon's headlamps. It appears to float in midair and we are utterly captivated. The thing is huge with wings the size of our front windshield. No doubt it is hunting for mice or rabbits. It hovers for what seems like minutes and then vanishes. We proceed up the road after it glides out of sight and drive through our gate. Strangely no dogs are there to greet us. Wilma and Pancho have been secured in the dog run so it stands to reason they are not running to our car but we have given Betty free range so it is odd that she is not there. Turns out she too is a stealth hunter for she has caught a rabbit on the front lawn and is proceeding to dismember and consume it in huge bone-snapping chomps. The sound is terrible and Mike makes his way with a shovel in an effort to take the thing away from her. Betty is not about to give up her prize and literally swallows the entire being nearly whole. Pancho and Wilma are let out of their pen and they know something has gone down and Betty's looking very self-satisfied. The next morning the dog run looks and smells awful, Betty having passed the thing in one huge, awful mess.

Following Betty's surgery we can tell she is itching to get on top of the doggy pecking order. We've liberated from her chronic pain and have done so with the best of intentions but it seems like it is backfiring.

One afternoon I am taking some flowers I had in the house in a vase down to our composter—yep, yet another investment and thing to lug stuff to and from—and I set the vase down to pull out the flowers. Wilma is always interested in anything I am doing and trots up and accidentally knocks the vase over and breaks it. I react and scold her and immediately regret what I have done. I can see Betty reacting too and it plays out in slow motion in my mind, Betty launching into a full out attack against Wilma. I scream, "No Betty," over and over. It is not as brutal as the time before but it was still terrifying because I am by myself and there is nothing I can do.

The muzzle goes back on Betty with due diligence. Not once does she ever confront or hassle Pancho, it is solely Wilma who is the target of her outbursts.

I ask Mike if he wants to build a fence down the back of the property like our vet had to do and Mike thinks that is crazy. We continue to keep them separated, leaving Betty out more in the evening by herself and Pancho and Wilma tucked in the dog run. In some ways this seems to further embolden Betty, she seems to see this as her getting greater preferential treatment. Every time now with the muzzle on her she goes after Wilma. It becomes exhausting and we are constantly on pins and needles. I make an effort to ask friends if they would be willing to take Betty just wanting to put an end to the fighting but we have no takers. Mike and I resort to what we call, "you go this way and I'll go that way." We literally yell over the house and across the yard to let one another know it is safe to release one dog, the other safely walked around the house and now secured inside the dog run so as to limit physical contact. The whole ordeal is exhausting but we feel trapped and want to keep our pets so we just do it, no matter how inconvenient and crazy the whole thing seems.

We manage to go on a few mini-vacations during this entire ordeal, leaving the dog's care with our *professional* pet sitter. We start to question her street smarts however when we return from a quick trip to Cabo San Lucas and upon opening our swing gate find a chair she had placed inside the gate moving inward and becoming wedged under the gate as it tries to open. Apparently she could not get the gate to open for her as she tried to leave the property and rather than resorting to climbing over the pedestrian gate which was small and stable, she moved a chair over to the fifteen foot swing gate and climbed over that thinking we would see the chair somehow and move it. The motor stalls and the gate sags making our mini-vacation that includes costly pet sitting fees even more expensive.

*****

I fully admit I carry my decorating obsession for the Santa Fe style too far. Plus I am the type of person when I make up my mind to do something I do it big and all at once. I have now painted the interior of our home with sand paint in a neutral beige color with spice colored accents and have purchased an eight-by-eight foot southwest desert scene to hang on the wall in the family room. I continue to spend and decorate as if money is no object at all and the fact that our home has gone up in value and we have refinanced, I feel rich via home equity. I keep looking at our ceilings and telling Mike how I would like some beams installed to mirror the vigas, or large wooden beams, you see in the pueblo style homes in New Mexico. Mike tells me that there is a company that makes faux beams for restaurants and large business interiors that might be willing to do what I want. I contact them and fax them a schematic and the color choice I want. A guy comes out to confirm measurements and $4000 later we have four huge beams on order. In the meantime we rip out all the carpeting in our house and have a terracotta color ceramic tile laid down throughout. We also contract for an above ground pool and deck and more concrete to be set around the pool area in addition to a vinyl patio cover off the family room and our bedroom. We are balancing a lot of home improvements and changes all at once.

Digging to put in the pool

Our above ground pool installed

Our cozy family room after much of the remodel

A patio cover to keep us cool

With most of the furniture we own stacked in our two back bedrooms, the installation for the beams begins. It is a nightmare. The installation crew is unreliable and they don't show up anywhere near the time span promised. They make a mess inside the house, leaving glue and debris. I call the business to complain, clarifying that this is someone's home that is occupied, not a construction site where shit can be left everywhere. They apologize and the next day I arrive home from work to find they had come and left the back door standing wide open. It is a painful process but finally they are done and we are able to reclaim the living room, family room and kitchen where the beams are installed. It looks pretty darn good.

Summer of 2003 all these changes are complete and we simply want to enjoy our place. My cousin and her husband and son come out to spend the Fourth of July weekend with us. They come out on a Friday and will stay two nights with us. Mike, the "grill master" cooks up a meal of carne asada chicken, corn on the cob, and potatoes. We pair it with salad and bread and sit out under the patio cover and take in the view and later the fireworks. I tell everyone to head down the road for a better view of the sky show while I clean up the kitchen. Wilma and Pancho are out and Betty is in the dog run. In the short time that Mike and our guests are gone, Betty ravages the screen leading into our bathroom from her dog run and leaves it in shreds. Wilma is at the backdoor whining to come in. Both dogs are terrified of the firework booms and are attempting to claw their way into the house. It's always something.

On Saturday morning I make huevos rancheros and we spend the day drinking margaritas, eating chips and salsa, listening to music and playing in the pool. My cousin's son Ryan is ten years old at this time and he heads into the house to use the restroom. He no sooner comes back out to the pool and we hear this horrific crash. It is one of the faux beams and it is lying cracked down the middle of the family room floor. Had it happened any sooner it could have killed him. I frantically search to make sure the cats are okay. Mahalo is fine but I cannot find Rally. Finally I find him behind the washing machine. He is trembling and absolutely terrified. We are beyond upset and immediately call the company and leave a very terse and direct voicemail that in no uncertain terms we want someone out to our home on Monday and we want the thing repaired and damages paid.

We all finally calm down and manage to enjoy the rest of our afternoon and evening.

In the wee hours of the next morning Mike gets up early to let the dogs out of their pen. He breaks protocol and Betty is not muzzled and she seizes the opportunity to provoke another fight. He's screaming and the next thing I know I'm outside too screaming at the top of my lungs both at the dogs and at Mike. My cousin and her family are now up as well and they cannot believe what they have just witnessed.

"You guys don't need to put up with this," my cousin tells us. "You have done everything you can for these dogs but you need to get rid of one of them. This is not healthy for you or them."

We immediately know she is right. It is the truth we have known for so long but did not have the heart to face—an agonizing choice, a decision no one should ever have to face or make. Somehow we manage to muddle through the morning until my cousin leaves and then Mike and I sit down to face what we need to do head on. There is anger and frustration, then grief and worry. We shed a ton of tears.

On Monday I handle the beam ordeal that presently seems minor in comparison to the grander picture of getting Betty in a shelter immediately for placement in another home. I call Tami to let her know that we need to separate the girls and why and she completely understands. Fortunately I have done some fundraising for the local animal shelter that is just reopening in a new location following the fire that destroyed the old one and I know the director. I call him and explain the entire situation and let him know I need a huge favor. Can he please work to find Betty a new home where she can be the only dog? He agrees to help us and tells us we can drop off Betty the following Saturday when the place will be prepared to receive animals. We are both heartbroken and yet hopeful all week, hoping that Betty will find herself a wonderful home where she can blossom and not feel like she has to constantly fight to be number one. We take her to the shelter with a pile of treats and toys and say our goodbyes to her and drive away, tearful and yet relieved too.

A sense of calm falls over our home following Betty's departure. Mike shares with me how stressful the entire ordeal was on him, never knowing when Betty might react.

"We had to do it," he tells me. "It was affecting our relationship too."

"I know, but it still hurts," I say.

"It was never Wilma's fault. Betty was always the instigator."

"I know," I say. "I know it is wrong to say it, but she will always be my favorite."

A month later I call to find out how Betty is doing. I am told that the shelter euthanized her. I feel guilty and totally devastated.

"But you said you would work to place her in a home," I cried when I spoke the director. "I wouldn't have left her here if I thought you would do that."

"Lori, we did place her, but it didn't work out and she just went nuts in the shelter and started nipping the staff. Her behavior was not acceptable and we can't place a risky pet."

The fights, the anxiety, the constant upkeep, none of that made any difference when he told me this. It is just one of those irreversible decisions you have to learn to try and accept and then move on with life. It is one decision I regret to this day, but I could never have foreseen the dreadful outcome.

Rest in Peace Betty

Ten

What are the Odds?

The daily newspaper Mike has delivered to the house says that there is a possible cancer cluster in Valley Center. A number of children and pets both have been diagnosed all within close proximity to us. We figure this must have to do with all pesticides that are frequently sprayed on the crops and we are concerned.

"This isn't good news for us or the community," Mike says. "Can you imagine trying to sell our home with this going on?"

We have no intentions of selling or moving so that isn't a huge concern, but we are worried for those who have become ill and want to know the extent of it.

Strangely, the news becomes diverted off this topic within a few short weeks and onto a possible medfly infestation. So now this means there will be aerial spraying of a pesticide. It defies logic. We run into our pet sitter and she tells us she is starting a class action suit against the spraying; she has kids and she is worried about their health. "I had the solution they are spraying tested," she said, "And it contains a toxic chemical that they are telling the public is not being used."

Sure enough I am outside hand watering my potted plants and some of our thirstier plants on the bank, and I hear the buzz of a small plane. I didn't expect them to spray directly over my home. I do have some fruit trees, but it isn't commercial and I did not agree to spraying, but sure enough over it comes releasing a supposed *natural* insect deterrent. Apparently they are going to douse all the vegetation within a certain radius of the infestation outbreak whether we have agreed to it or not. I bring Pancho and Wilma into the garage and close our windows.

"This could possibly be worse than a cancer cluster," I say. "Now our home lies in the path of aerial insecticide spraying."

The crop duster comes and goes over a series of weeks and then the spraying finally comes to an end.

Then as if we need more negative publicity there is an outbreak of Newcastle disease at all the local poultry farms—including the one where we get our fresh eggs. The solution to stop the spread of this contagious bird virus is to slaughter all these chickens and so they do. They aren't delicate about it and birds are thrown live into wood chippers. It's absolutely terrible and I recommit to becoming a vegetarian again.

Even with Betty gone and the household under a more placid mood, I seem to be more stressed than ever. I was so excited to get the plants and the pool and all the trappings of our very large home, but now I feel like I spend much more time maintaining and not very much time enjoying. Its as if the process of creation was exciting because it felt productive and I felt a sense of accomplishment, but now having to keep this whole thing going is brutal. Plus work is so tough, I have several employees that report to me that are poor performers and I am told that if I manage them out of the organization I will not get replacements for their positions. And I have brought incredible debt upon myself, having to have all these things that I can't do anything but endure this. I am trapped.

I continue to exercise in the morning in the home gym we have installed and either take the dogs for a walk or take a swim during the warm summer months in the evenings. I'm trying to keep us both healthy by preparing nutritious meals for dinner but more often than not it is quick prep Monday through Friday and that isn't always the most wholesome of choices. We revert to frozen pizza, lasagna, enchiladas—a lot of heavy, fattening foods. We both put on a few more pounds of weight than fit our smaller frames.

Weekends I try to sleep in. In fact, it is my refuge and I have a harder and harder time getting out of bed on Saturdays and Sundays. Mike puts the kibosh on this by letting Rally and Mahalo into our room. Rally is a big fat yellow tabby that loves nothing more than to paddy cake my head and he does so with gusto and lots of noise. How can I get mad?

Cute little Rally-Bob

Rally stays cozy by the fire

Mahalo checks out something of interest outside

In October Mike and I go to Las Vegas for the weekend on a trip he has won for doing such an outstanding sales job for his company. The company flies us there and puts us up in the hotel Paris. We have a great time. We enjoy the camaraderie of his coworkers, have some terrific meals, and manage to go to a concert featuring Aerosmith and KISS. On Sunday morning we get transportation to the airport to fly home and are waiting to board our plane when we hear that our flight has been canceled.

"That's strange," I say to Mike.

A coworker is on his cell phone and looks over at us when he is done and tells us that San Diego is on fire.

"What?" we ask.

"The entire county has fires, they are everywhere and the smoke is so bad that they have shut down all flights. Traffic control can't see through all the smoke," he tells us.

We learn that one of the fires is centered where we live and that our community has been evacuated.

"The pets!" I cry to Mike.

I call my dad to confirm what is going on as he lives in San Diego and sure enough Valley Center is on fire. I immediately call our pet sitter and she tells me that she did not evacuate the dogs and cats. She cannot tell me if they are dead or alive. I'm hysterical and worried beyond disbelief. She chose to prioritize some other pets and by the time she could go to our home, they would not let her past the barricades.

"Let's rent a car and get out of here," Mike's coworker says.

We get in the rental line and luck out with one of the last vehicles available. It is a large SUV and there are six of us who will travel together back to San Diego. In normal traffic the drive should be around six hours. We figure we will be home early evening. We weren't even close. Thousands of cars are attempting the same drive. Freeways are closed, mountain passes glow a vibrant orange, traffic barely moves. We finally pull off early evening to get a bite to eat. One of the people in our car is saying that there have been a lot of homes and some people burned in our town. I can't eat I am so upset and I want to punch the living crap out of this woman. Mike works hard to keep me calm.

Hours and hours pass and because Mike and I live the furthest out we are designated to drop the two couples off at their respective places before we can finally go home. It's 3:00 am and we come up the Old Castle Road grade to get to our house. We reach a fire department blockade and talk to the officer on duty. He tells us where we want to go has been evacuated but the fire is no longer burning directly there so he will allow us to drive through, get our animals, and then tells us we need to immediately leave once we secure our pets.

Mike drives on and continues down the country road towards our place. The air is so smoky and gray but there is a glimmer of moonlight. We see a car completely burnt out at the side of the road a half-mile from our place. I keep saying, "Oh my God, oh my God," over and over and I am shaking so hard my teeth are rattling. We come to our street and make the turn down the ravine where we saw the owl, and the house at the foot of our street on the left is gone, it has been destroyed by fire. We continue up our street and Mike lets out a sigh of relief. There are four houses standing. Our solar powered swing gate opens and two very happy but weary dogs greet us. Mike says he'll back out his truck so we can load the dogs and get the cats and get out of there.

"I'm not going anywhere," I tell him. "The fire has left and I am staying here."

We can see the orange glow several ridges over at the point where it drops down onto the Rincon Indian Reservation. This is where one of the casinos was recently built. There is smoldering everywhere but our immediate property is clear of combustible materials and I don't want to leave.

Mike agrees with me and we grab hoses and start watering down the roof of our house and all the vegetation that surrounds it just in case there are blowing embers. It is very warm out, the hot Santa Ana winds spreading the wildfire away from us, not towards us.

All our neighbors are gone and the place is so eerie and devoid. We can't open the windows because of the smoke and the inside of the house is stifling hot. We have no electricity and therefore cannot run fans or air. We've been up for 24 hours and take turns napping while the other stands guard, watching for any turn in the fires.

Midmorning we see the fire department down our country road treating embers so they don't roar to life again. They come up our road and Wilma and Pancho chase their truck along the fence line. They wave at us and are surprised to see us there but don't tell us to leave.

My dad had given us a gadget for Christmas the prior year that at the time seemed silly but is now a lifesaver. It is an emergency television/radio/lamp/compass all rolled into one. Mike is able to tune into the television and pick up a local station via antennae. We get the gist of the extent of the fires and they literally are everywhere. Firefighters have come into the county from all over the country. The fire closest to our home is being called the Paradise Fire and is allegedly started by arson on the nearby Indian reservation. Several neighbors on nearby streets lost their lives because of this fire, and many lost their pets, and homes. We are beside ourselves with grief.

"We're going to need ice for our food," Mike tells me. He is planning on taking his personal truck into nearby Escondido and dealing with the rental car later. Before he leaves I call our pet sitter to let her know we are home and that the pets are safe. She is upset with herself for leaving them when they were in her charge so I don't make matters worse with my anger even though I agree it was completely irresponsible.

While Mike is gone I visit with the dogs that are lying in the garage trying to find reprieve from the choking smoke and heat. There is little light in the garage except for a few windowed slits that appear in the shape of a peacock fan on the front of the garage door. I hear a vehicle come up the road and stop in front of our gate. Then I see I light being shined through the slits into the garage. "Interesting," I say to myself. I roll up the garage door by hand and the dogs go charging out at the car. A man with long hair holds out a badge and tells me his is with the Drug Enforcement Agency and they are lending a hand with law enforcement since most of the homes in the area are evacuated and thus vulnerable to theft.

"You've got the best deterrent against thieves right there," he says pointing at the dogs as they bark at him through the gate. "Be careful, and if you see anyone around who shouldn't be here, please give us a call."

The two men hand me their card and drive away and suddenly I feel fear. The fires made me nervous, but now I feel even more vulnerable. We only have one cell phone and Mike has taken it with him so that the battery can be recharged as he drives.

When Mike returns I tell him about the guys from the DEA and he smiles at the dogs, proud that they are doing their jobs well. We take two coolers from the garage and load them with ice and put the salvageable refrigerated items inside along with some drinks to get them cold. We assume everything in the freezer will need to be tossed since the stuff will be long thawed before we see electricity again.

We are outside wetting the vegetation out front again, not just because of the threat of fire, but more so from the incessant heat. Another car comes up with a toothless guy and a couple of kids with him. "The fires are bad," he says. "Are you guys going to stay here?" he asks us.

"Yeah, we're staying and we are also keeping an eye on our neighbor's homes too." Mike tells the guy. The guy drives away and we don't see him again.

Mike and I both phone our employers and let them know we'll be back in a few days. The fires are too much of a threat and we're concerned about leaving our property unattended. I attempt to sweep the back patio of ash and clean

76

the pool and realize I will need to clean that pool another ten times before it becomes clean. By the third day after the fire began both our electricity and the neighbors return and Mike and I feel secure enough to head back to work. I'm a nervous wreck and have a hard time keeping my composure. I am one of the lucky ones but so much devastation so close does something to one's psyche. That evening Mike and I are both crying as we return to Valley Center and see the main drag in the center of town littered with emergency response and fire vehicles. Firefighters and responders to whom we will be eternally grateful, from all over the country, working in our little town to save lives and structures; they are heroes all. We take every opportunity to wave to them and thank them.

An odd sense of normalcy returns to Valley Center and our lives. The earth is scorched all around us and we see that more structures were lost than we had originally observed, and many much too close to our home for comfort. Our neighbors relive the night of the fire, the evacuation, the terror through their shared stories and accounts as we see them and discuss it all over the fence lines. The shift of the wind is literally what spared us all the complete loss of everything.

*****

My Mother-in-law Jackie and her husband Howard are coming to visit. They are wonderful people and we see them every few years either in Vermont, or in San Diego. This time they are driving their RV across the country and plan to spend some time touring the Southwest. They are finally making their way to San Diego since having been delayed by the fires. I am still working to remove the ash from our pool and patio cover when they arrive. They have been watching the media coverage of the fires but it simply could not prepare them for the devastation in real life.

Stan and Cindy decide to host a dinner for the neighborhood and include Darlene, an elderly woman who lives alone with her dog Trixie up at the corner intersection of our street. We learn that Jesus and Stan took control during the evacuation and made sure that Paula, who is now a widow, and Darlene got safely out too. Everyone took their pets but there was not enough time or resources to safely retrieve our pets or Popeye. Fortunately Popeye is fine. They explain how the fire was jumping the road and they were forced to drive through the flames in a caravan. Then, when the meal is finished, Stan and Cindy drop a bombshell and announce to us that they are planning to sell their home and move. They are not moving as a result of the fires, but rather Stan has received a promotion and it is in the Los Angeles area. We are all so saddened.

Mike's mom and step-dad stay for a month and we have a lovely time. Slowly the ash and smell of smoke dissipates. Time does heal wounds and things eventually return to normal in our world. By the time Jackie and Howard leave to make the drive back to Vermont the fire trucks are gone from the community and all the backcountry fires are out.

Soon another holiday season is upon us and we celebrate friends, family and our good fortune. So blessed by so many things.

We aren't sure if it is the stress of the fires that exacerbates Rally's decline but he becomes very ill right after Christmas. He goes from fourteen pounds to six or seven in a matter of a few months. We look at him one Sunday morning and both agree it is time to relieve him before the pain and suffering become amplified. We have no way of really knowing what he feels at this point, but he is unstable on his feet, one of his pupils is massively dilated and he vomits water—so this can't be good. We take him to the emergency vet and he is euthanized in my arms. I cry and cry. Saying "goodbye" to another of our beloved pets breaks our hearts.

Lori Colt

Rest in Peace Rally

Eleven

Of Gazanias and ATV's

Stan and Cindy sell their home quickly and in late fall a family moves in next door. This time Mike and I are pulling the antics of Eddie, though with a bit more panache and subtleness than riding our bikes in circles around our house. They are a young couple, the woman, Tina *very* young, and the guy, Gerald appears to be in his thirties. They have one infant and another in the oven. They like toys. A plethora of ATVs, motorcycles and a large RV litter their driveway.

They are there a few weeks when the wife Tina invites me, and the other women on the street, to a candle party she is hosting. She seems nice enough and she has done a wonderful job of decorating the interior of their home—this is a pleasant and unexpected surprise since I was making a judgment on her character based on what I had seen in the driveway. I guess I was expecting something tacky with the combination of her age and the motorcycles, but it is tastefully done. Tina tells me that Gerald is in a rock band and the band plans to practice at their house a few times a month. I'm not super excited about it, valuing the quiet, but what can I say?

Tina delivers her baby not long hereafter and they have a lot of visitors coming and going. Tina's father breeds chocolate Labradors and gives them a puppy for their sons to grow up with and enjoy. They tell us the puppy's name is Latté and he is adorable. For a few months we see Gerald and his toddler son playing with the puppy outside. Tina spends most of her time inside so we don't see her often. We hear the band once or twice but they usually knock off early so we tolerate it.

By January 2004 two things are dead—many of our free gazanias and the marriage of our new young neighbors. We really didn't see either of these things coming and both have a profound impact on the quality of our life.

*****

Mike and I are both so tired of the constant upkeep of our yard by now. I thought a drought tolerant and cactus garden with some flowers would have been easy but we find we work more in the yard on weekends than we enjoy it and the pool upkeep is constant. We are having a wet winter and so I've had a number of evenings where I drive home from work in the pounding rain and have to hook up a reverse pump to empty some of the water out of the pool. I divert the water down the dry riverbed and it serves to further water the sprouting weeds. Now we have a combination of new mustard weed and spent, brown gazanias that have become unsightly. I ask Mike if he can hire a few day workers for the weekend to help us with the weeding. We had a gardener we used for a few years since we put the yard in. He was unreliable at best. We'd leave the money under the front door mat for him, giving him a special gate code to get in, and he'd take the money, do a part of the job, and then not show up for a while to complete the rest of the task—always an excuse for why he couldn't to a six hour day all at once. He was very nice and convincing and when he was here and actually *worked,* he did a decent job, it was the other times that got on our nerves—the times of purported family issues, car problems and the litany of other lame excuses one chooses to use. In fact once we received a phone call from him about nine months after Mike had called him to ask him to come do some work. "Hello Mike, it is Fernando. I got your message and I can come to your place next Tuesday," he said in his thick Hispanic accent. Now that was funny. We changed the gate code so he no longer had access. He even had the audacity to tell our neighbor Jesus that we had not paid him which was not true and made us really mad.

Mike picks up two guys at the gas station near our home. He has hired one of them before but it is always strange to have people you don't really know come onto your property to work. We never had a problem so we felt safe enough. We put Mexican music on for them and treat them to lunch. I go to Snoopy's—the very *slow* fast good drive thru—and get them both carne asada burritos and papas (French fries). At the end of the day Mike drives them back to Escondido where they live so they don't need to thumb a ride. We hire them twice that month for two weekends and spend $600. We feel that cash expenditure and Mike says, "the *free* gazanias weren't such a good deal after all."

We began to hear loud arguing from Tina and Gerald's house below us. It sounds intense and angry. Either things are not going well with them or they are very loud communicators. A moving van shows up and by February Gerald mentions to Mike that Tina has filed for divorce and moved out.

The puppy gets relegated to Popeye's old horse pen and he is not happy to be left alone so often. He howls and cries all the time, night and day. We think Gerald must be deaf. Soon the weekends consist of around ten cars descending on Gerald's residence on a Friday night, a loud party including his band that goes until late in the evening, and then Saturday no movement at all. Latté is going crazy in the morning and we wonder if he has even been fed. I toss food and toys into his pen and he delights in the attention and snacks. By Saturday afternoon, the stupor appears to wear off and the ATVs and motorcycles fire up and go up and down our street and onto the nearby roads and hills. We are both annoyed and pissed. "What is with all the noise?"

Mike talks to Gerald to let him know how his band, dog and parties are impacting the neighborhood. "Our bedroom is right there," Mike says as he points to the room we sleep in perched at the edge of the property just above Gerald's place.

"I can't make noise in the suburbs," Gerald says. "That's why I moved out here. I want space to do the things I enjoy like playing music, riding my motorcycle and having a dog."

Impasse.

*****

We have a solar blanket on our pool in an effort to keep the water of our unheated pool warm. By Memorial Day it is warm enough to get in during the day. We've got the day off today and are taking time to swim and relax on our deck. Jesus' son Benjamin is seventeen now and very much the obstinate teenager according to his parents. He has been kicked out of school for bringing a knife onto campus and has become argumentative and uncooperative. Jesus wants to see him go into the Navy or Marines to give him discipline. He feels there is no respect and he has all but given up. Benjamin comes home that Monday on a motorcycle and proceeds to race up and down and all around his backyard kicking up waves of dust that fall on the pool deck and us, and making a terrible racket.

"So much for enjoying our afternoon and the pool. Now we have surround sound noise," Mike says. We're furious.

The following week is very intense at work, followed by evenings of Latté howling and Benjamin racing back and forth on his motorcycle. I feel like I am going to crack in half. By Thursday I come home and I am so worked up I throw my briefcase on the kitchen island and say to Mike, "I can't do this anymore. I hate my job and I hate maintaining this property and I hate all the noise we have in our neighborhood now."

"What do you want to do?" he asks me.

"I want to move, I want to live somewhere where I can get a stupid job and I'm not spending every single second maintaining stuff or paying someone to maintain our stuff."

"Okay. I don't want to see you like this. This isn't worth it. Let's figure out a plan and we'll sell this place and move. Then you can quit your job and find something you like. You just need to hang on until you are vested in your pension. You will regret it later if you don't."

I am not happy about delaying solace but I know Mike is right. At the same time, I am profoundly relieved that Mike has put us, me, ahead of this house. I will be vested in my companies' pension by fall so now it is just a matter of figuring out our plan.

As a diversion I take up winemaking. Maybe its because I am already drinking more wine than I should when I get home from work—a terrible coping mechanism—but what the heck. I find a wine making book and I really get into it. The grape vines we planted aren't really ready and there wouldn't be enough anyways so I make wine with other fruits. I make three batches:

apricot, strawberry and raisin. I save all my wine bottles and friends save them for me too. I've got food grade vats for the fermenting fruit and I learn the chemistry to test and refine the wines as they evolve. The house smells like yeast and other organic smells and the wine gets stored in one of the spare closets so it can rest quietly and coolly and complete its transformation. I decide I need a label for my wine and we use a photo of Pancho and Wilma, seated near our grapevines with two glasses of wine on a table next to them. The label is called "Double Dog Haze." Mike helps me bottle the wine when it is ready and we yield fifteen gallons total, five gallons of each flavor. The wine will need time to settle in the bottles but we both look forward to sampling and sharing them when they are ready.

Image we used for our double dog haze wine label

Twelve

Do You Want to Go to Santa Fe?

In June we plan a trip to visit Vermont family.

Mike and I with his mom Jackie and step-dad Howard in Grand Isle, VT

From left: Bro-in-law Sam, niece Emily, Mike's sis Patty,
Mike, Me, mom Jackie, step-dad Howard

"What if we only stay in Vermont for four days and then fly to Sequim, Washington to see if this might be a good place for us to move to?" Mike asks me. He's been reading lots of *good places to live* articles and has been impressed with what he has read in the Pacific Northwest. He is smitten by the photos he's seen, the Olympic National Forest, the proximity to Canada, seafood—a biggie for my New Englander husband, small town feel, affordable housing and decent weather in the banana belt of Washington state. In the meantime, I am advocating for Santa Fe since I am still completely in love with the mystique of the town, the culture, history and décor.

"Sure, that sounds good," I say, willing to look at a second option.

Our trip to visit family is terrific, as are all our trips to New England. Mike's mom comes from a huge French-Canadian family and I always enjoy spending time with his immediate family, sister, aunts, uncles and cousins. They are a crazy bunch with olive skin, small eyes and enormous hearts.

We leave Burlington and fly to Seattle, Washington where we rent a car and after a ferry ride across the river, drive to Sequim. They are having an unseasonable heat wave and it is very hot. The place we stay in should be called the "Red Raunch Inn" instead of its *real* name because the air conditioner is broken and with 100-degree heat their pet-friendly policy leaves us with a dirty, stained and very smelly room. The place is gross and they go ahead and charge us for the second night even though we complain about the quality and don't plan to stay there a second night. While we are there we check out the Dungeness Spit—the longest skinny land stretch in North America that teams with sea lions, the lighthouse at the end of the spit and the local lavender farms. We eat seafood and local lemon cake. Everyone in the town has blue hair and there isn't much to do—if I was 70 or older I might think differently. I'm not impressed and tell Mike so. While we are there we also look at Port Angeles and Port Townsend, both other possibilities on Mike's list. The area just isn't doing much for me. We spend one final night in Seattle and have a great time. We love the urban feel and fantasize what it would be like in a Seattle downtown high rise but both know the gray skies would be tough and what the heck would we do with two big dogs in a high rise? I have one last bite of salmon on a bagel at the airport before we leave and wind up with a severe case of food poisoning. At this point

I'm not sure if I'll ever move, sure I am going to die right then and there in Valley Center.

Mike on the Dungeness Spit in Washington

We discuss Santa Fe and Mike does some research on jobs, cost of living, home prices, crime, etc. We decide Santa Fe it is and list our home on the first day of August with a husband and wife realtor team. Home sales are sky high right now and the realtors give us a hopeful selling price they aim to meet. The first week other realtors come to our home in order to become familiar with our property in case they have a prospective buyer. Anyone who has been through the selling of their home understands the continuous stress of keeping their home perfect, the yard perfect, the interior staged, and the worry over pets getting loose.

Buy my cute home please

87

$679,900 - $719,900

VALLEY CENTER, CA 92082

*JASMINE MODEL *JUST BUILT IN 1999 *2.16 ACRES *4 BEDROOMS *2 BATH
*3 CAR GARAGE * 2435 SQUARE FEET *PANORAMIC MOUNTAIN VIEWS

- Impressive gated, solar-powered entry to property
- Dramatic interior presentation   model perfect
- Ceiling fans throughout
- Designer faux wood beams accent ceilings
- Built in media center in oversized family room
- Numerous skylights brighten the interior
- Art niche adds an architectural touch
- Large laundry room with sink and decorator tile
- Sunny breakfast nook makes mornings bright
- Chef s kitchen with abundant cabinetry and gourmet preparation island
- Dual-sided stone fireplace warms living and family rooms
- Privately located at the end of a quite country road.

- Dual-glazed windows for energy efficiency
- Wood-trimmed sills, wood blinds
- Custom designer tile flooring   quality accents this home!
- Arched doorways create a designer feel
- Even the pooch has a new home   a separate dog kennel
- Faux wood patio cover for easy maintenance
- Splashy above-ground gated pool, with large lounging deck
- Artistically designed water-wise landscaping adds greatly to the ambiance
- Rock trails wind through grapes vines, various variety of family fruit trees, stunning cactus and succulent collection
- Finished 3car garage includes shelving and cabinets

At first we keep Wilma and Pancho locked in their dog pen all day and give our realtors their own gate code to provide to other realtors. I put some signs I found at a specialty shop on all the exterior door handles reminding visitors not to let the cat out. We stage the house, making sure every nook and cranny is clean and shiny. We put on light jazz music and leave lights on. We get a few people who come and are interested but some don't like the remoteness, or the fact that our house is all tile, or a variety of other things. I feel bad for the dogs as they are cooped up all day and then only get out a few hours before we herd them back in their pen for the evening. Finally after four weeks of this and very few prospects I tell the realtor wife that we are going to keep the dogs out and that we'd like her to call us the day before if she, or any other broker, has a prospective client who wants to see our place so we can lock the dogs up in that case. A few more weeks go by and we are told a client who was only there for the day *would have gone to see the house had they not needed to give a days notice.* C'est la vie.

*****

It is now early October and I am fully vested in my employer's pension plan and 401K. I really want to quit my job and sell the house. Our realtor wife tells us another realtor is bringing by a couple and the husband's mother to see our place. They like the description on the ad that has been running and they have targeted Valley Center as where they want to live. We receive a second call a few days later and they want to see the house again. We completely stage the place and it looks fantastic. When we put our tile flooring and patio cover on last year Mike had stereo wires run under the flooring and inside the legs of the patio cover so we have speakers throughout. We have light jazz music on and set up wine, glasses, and a cracker and cheese plate with a note telling them to take their time and enjoy themselves. We jump in my Volkswagon beetle and drive to the adjacent country road and sit with binoculars in hand so we can check out the goings on while they are there. We catch a few short glimpses of them, see doors open and close, and we fill our minds with a happy ending full of dollar signs.

The next day we receive an offer from their realtor. It is $10,000 less than what we really wanted so we counter. This goes on twice over the course of a week and they come back with the number we want, contracting to pay us much more for the property than we actually spent when we bought it. We enter into a 30-day escrow. We are beyond excited but I am also on pins and needles with anxiety of the things that could go wrong. Mike and I laugh because we learn one of the things they like most about our place is the southwest feel of it and the *maintenance-free* cactus yard.

Mike starts bringing home packing boxes from work and we make arrangements to fly to Santa Fe over a three-day weekend. Throughout all of this we have maintained contact with a realtor named Joyce in Santa Fe, and have told her we are interested particularly in an area called Eldorado. It sounds like a cool place. The real estate materials indicate Eldorado has temperate weather with mild winters, several acres properties, CC&Rs so folks can't have purple house or run down yards, one of the largest home-studio artist communities in the country, and it isn't really a planned development—the houses are all individually built so that ones home doesn't look like every other one of the block—except that they are all painted varying shades of brown.

We give Joyce the dates when we will be there so she can set up appointments for us to see the houses we are interested in. Just for the heck of it Mike contacts a guy who ran an advertisement in the local Eldorado paper and is selling his house by owner. It isn't on the multiple listings so we don't see an image of it, but the description sounds good. It's much smaller than our existing house and that appeals to us both. We decide to see it the first night we are there just to have it in mind for comparison.

Front courtyard to our Santa Fe home

We meet the owners John and Teresa that first night and we love their little house. It is a third of the size of our Valley Center home and it is the adobe style we love, with real vigas on the ceilings and nichos in the walls inside the house. We sit outside for a short time on the back patio that overlooks the greenbelt, well actually brown belt because it is now autumn. There is no yard really to speak of it; is all natural vegetation which has tremendous appeal. The vista is grand and a series of mountain chains face the house from the south, west and east. We spend a good half hour there and then thank John and Teresa for their time when we are finished.

"Who knows," Mike says to John, "we may be back before the weekend is over to buy your house."

On Saturday we meet up with Joyce who is a former San Diegan herself, and she carts us all over the place in Eldorado. She drives us in her swanky black Mercedes up and down the community's network of dirt roads. We see a dozen properties in our price range and none even come close to the house we looked at last night. Mike tells me under his breath at about the fifth place, "I don't even need to see any more of these homes. All of these look like the owners don't even care— dishes in the sink, dirt, and filth. If they are willing to leave their counters and bathrooms in this state of mess, what general maintenance things are they not doing? I'm not seeing any pride of ownership in relation to the house we looked at last night."

I say, "Yeah, I agree, but we owe it to ourselves to be really sure. This is a huge move so let's see the rest of the homes she has lined up for us today."

Joyce drops us off at our hotel that afternoon and we immediately turn around and jump in our rental car and drive back to Eldorado. We drive up and down the street of the first house imagining what it would be like to live there. "Its small, but it will work, and that is what we wanted. Less to maintain, and it would definitely be a *lifestyle change*," Mike tells me.

I agree with him and he phones John to see if we can come back over on Sunday morning to discuss buying their place, then we call Joyce to thank her for her time and let her know we are tacking in a different direction. We go out that night in Santa Fe and celebrate with a nice dinner, excited to know we might be one step closer to leaving San Diego and moving into a home that we can buy with cash.

Sunday we agree on a price and Monday we sign the contract with John and Teresa, the offer is contingent on the selling of our home in Valley Center. We fly back to San Diego feeling lighter and excited, so hopeful that all the small details will fall into place.

It's a mini-winter wonderland

We're down to two weeks before the escrow is to close on the Valley Center home. I've started bringing Wilma and Pancho alternately to doggy day care at $35 per pop. I want to make sure that there is a place that they can stay while we exit our existing home and before we make the drive to Santa Fe since we'll be staying with my dad during that time and his yard isn't equipped to handle two large, rambunctious dogs. We are calculating ten to fourteen days where they will need to be housed and we want to make sure the transition is conflict free. With Wilma's history and their general lack of socialization with other dogs I bite my nails each time I drop them off. But, the day care owner said they both did fine so I am glad I took the time to get them somewhat acclimated.

We've gone ahead and sold more than half of our furniture since our new home is so much smaller. We say goodbye to our living room set—the lovely cream-colored leather sofas and the faux marble tables we bought when we first purchased our Scripp's Ranch home. We say adios to our guest bedroom furniture—the set I bought from my aunt that originated from Nantucket and was handmade and hand-painted in the early 1900's. We sell the barstools we had made especially for our Valley Center home center island in the kitchen. And we say *see ya* to Wilma's favorite cement patio set we bought so recently, knowing it would be too heavy to move to New Mexico.

The Cape Cod guest room

Bye-bye Cape Cod guest room in Valley Center

Parting with our belongings, and having already given notice at work, I'm sick with anxiety of what could go wrong to stop the sell, our dreams, and our move. My mind wanders to all kinds of things, *the what if this and what if that's.*

On Friday night Gerald is playing rock star again. I love music but this band is terrible. There are drums, guitars and amplifiers up the wazoo and all they are making is racket, not music. The singing even sucks. It's getting late and I'm tired and I just so damned sick of listening to the cacophony of noise emanating from his garage and I snap. I tell Mike, "I'm going to go down there and tell them to shut-up. I just can't take this anymore."

"No you won't," he says with a dare in his voice.

"Watch me," I say.

I change from my pajamas into street clothes and storm down there in a fit of rage. I bring a large flashlight and shine it through the small windows on the garage door and bang as hard as I can on the thing. I swear steam is coming out of my ears and I am shaking I'm so pissed. The music dies down as if the power plug has been pulled. *Whaaaaaannnnnn.*

"Shit, it's the cops," I hear one of the jerks say. I can smell Mary Jane and a huge puff of smoke rolls out of the garage as they pull up the door. Gerald is surprised to see me.

"Look, I am really tired of hearing you every Friday night. It's late and you are very loud, and you're keeping us awake," I tell him as my entire body shakes with fervor.

"By law I can play until ten o'clock," he says. Clearly he's been down this path before if he knows what the legal *turn that noise off* time is.

"You are keeping us awake and yes I will call the cops if you don't stop. I'm sick and tired of listening to all your noise. You're a lousy, inconsiderate neighbor," I add.

I march back up the hill to our place and I see Mike mirroring my walk along the edge of our property in shadow. He meets me at the front gate and congratulates me on my boldness.

"I was watching in case anything got out of hand," he tells me.

"Believe me," I say, "I am so mad these guys would have regretted it if they tried to pull anything on me." And I know this is true.

*****

We hire a moving service to transport all of our belongings to New Mexico—I've got multiple quotes to do this and am astonished how expensive it is. We hire movers out of Los Angeles who plan to load the truck and then take everything to a warehouse, offload it and store it for 14 days, and then reload and transport it when we are ready. This type of moving opens one up to things being lost and damaged because your stuff is being handled multiple times, but it is cheaper than paying for a container to sit there occupied so we go with it. We have packed everything ourselves and we have the movers come on the Friday escrow is to close to load up our stuff and then they will deliver it two weeks later to our home in Santa Fe. I've brought the dogs to the long-term doggy day care the prior day so that they will be out of the way of the movers. The dogs will remain at the long-term facility until the morning we leave to drive to Santa Fe. We'll be going to my dad's house tonight to live for the next two weeks, and then we'll pick up the dogs and drive to Santa Fe. Everything is on the truck by one o'clock when we get a call from the husband of our realtor team.

"There has been a slight glitch in the closing of escrow and it cannot be completed today. Escrow is being delayed until Tuesday since Monday is Veteran's Day.

"You're kidding, right?" I ask him.

"No, it will be fine. The account will fund on Tuesday. The Buyers have done everything necessary. This is a snafu at the bank but we still need you to bring the keys to the office for the new buyers. They are moving in this weekend."

This feels all wrong. I tell Mike what he just said and Mike responds, "Damn, we don't have our house or our stuff, and we don't have the money either."

We had planned to use the funded money for the check we are writing for the movers and they don't accept credit. It's a mad scramble to find the funds to cover the check but we manage by writing three separate checks to satisfy the payment.

The van leaves and Mike takes off to go to my dad's place. I stay and do a final cleaning, then toss the mop and remaining stuff into Jesus' dumpster, not wanting to transport a dirty old mop to Santa Fe. This time I do look in the review mirror as the L&M gate closes and I drive away. I'll miss this place even though it was work, work, work it holds history and memories and good times and some not-so-good times. I see the stains of hard work and dedication and sweat as my tires hug the road down our street for one last time. I shed a tear for what was but am excited for the future.

Thirteen

Let it Snow

My father and his wife Cheryle are very kind to let Mike and I, and Mahalo stay at their home for two weeks. During this time Mike gives his notice and both our jobs come to a close. It feels amazing to collect my final paycheck and get out of the toxic job I have been doing, to leave behind the negativity and management games. I have given a 30-day notice so that my employer will have plenty of time to get things in order and so I can train my replacement and I simply cannot wait to get out of there. My last day is on a Wednesday and my boss wants to take me out to lunch while I just want to say goodbye and leave. I explain I have things I need to wrap up before Friday so they hand me my final paycheck while I hand them my badge and keys and we part amicably. This gives me a few days to see friends and family one last time before we go. Mike meanwhile decides to work right up until the day we leave. People think we are nuts to go but we feel really optimistic about our future. Some people have told us that when you leave California, you can never come back. We are debt free and starting a new adventure where we do not know a soul and will have the opportunity to reinvent our lives. We are excited beyond words.

On our way out of San Diego County on Saturday morning we go to the doggy daycare place. Wilma and Pancho recognize Mike's truck the minute we pull up the road and we can see them, and an entourage of their twenty new doggy friends racing along the fence line, so excited and happy are they to see us. We pay the nice lady, Pancho says goodbye to his two-week girlfriend—a fling with a golden retriever, then he and Wilma jump in the camper shell and off we go on our new adventure to New Mexico.

I'm following behind Mike in my Volkswagon with Mahalo in a carrier beside me and we head out, planning to take a number of rest stops along the way and then stay overnight in Winslow, Arizona. We both have made sure we have ample music on hand and snacks—for both human and animal—and make our way out of California by midday. We cross the state line into Arizona and take a few breaks here and there. In Flagstaff we stop for yet another potty break and there is snow. The dogs have never seen this cold white stuff before and they are too confused and distracted to relieve themselves. As we continue on towards Winslow the snow is falling hard now and there is road construction. I'm a Southern California girl and I've never driven in anything trickier than a little rain so with a diverted road, center cement pilasters, and blinding snow I find myself humming at the top of my lungs trying to calm myself as I hurl through frozen sleet curtain of snow and passing semi trucks. My knuckles are white and I am filled with anxiety. Finally we arrive at our hotel and I am so grateful to park the car and get out for the night. We walk the dogs and feed them and then put them back in the camper shell where they will safely spend the night. I let Mahalo out of his carrier but leave him in the car so he can access his litter box. I feed him and then he tucks himself safely into his small cat bed for the night. Our night is sleepless, we're excited to get to our new home and anxious about the pets being left in our vehicles. We are eager to arrive at our new Santa Fe home in time to meet the movers the next day.

We're up with the sun the next morning. We take care of the dogs and cat and then heading due east we stare straight into sun for the first hour of the drive. Mahalo has had enough of being crated and tells me so on this second day of driving. He howls and carries on so much I think something must be wrong. I flag Mike to pull over and he unhappily accommodates me. I try to get Mahalo to use his box but I sense he is just restless so after fifteen minutes of cajoling its time to go back in his crate and we move on. It's a noisy ride on day two; Mahalo carries on like he is being tortured. Mike and I both honk our horns and wave at each other as we cross the New Mexico state line for good luck and then safely arrive into Santa Fe around noon on Sunday. The movers have been in cell phone contact and arrive not long after. It's very cold in Santa Fe and one of the movers asks if I can whip up some coffee. I laugh, because the coffee maker and coffee are buried somewhere in the 25 boxes marked, "kitchen." As a consolation I drive up to a place that is three miles from our new home and buy a pizza and some drinks. There are no streetlights in Eldorado and I get turned around, I have to make several U-turns until I find my way back to my new house.

We have no sooner finished the pizza and it starts to snow. Neither of these Los Angeles guys have prepared for snow so they are more than ready to say adios and make for their next assignment. Soon, Mike and I are left alone in our new place, the dogs nesting in the garage and Mahalo making his way through his new digs.

In the morning we wake up and there are six inches of the frozen white stuff on the ground outside and in the boughs of the junipers and it is very cold. The brochures we had read prior to deciding upon Santa Fe all said, *"Santa Fe has four mild seasons"* but that isn't the case this morning. Thanksgiving is soon upon us and another four inches arrives. By December we are in the single digits with a lot of snow. Our new neighbors tell us this is very unusual. Still Mike tells me one morning early on that he and the dogs have taken a vote and they are all moving back to San Diego. I laugh and he laughs but underneath it is a Vermonter who has experienced more snow than he wanted already in a lifetime and he isn't excited about experiencing more.

Fourteen

I'll be there on Thursday

New Mexico really is just a newer version of Mexico but it resides in the United States. It feels like that often as we try to work with local contractors to make modifications and improve the property to our liking. We find the state doesn't have a lot of competition and we are held a captive audience. This comes as a big adjustment to us since we're accustomed to choices—getting several bids on a job before we decide on a contractor. For instance, we need a fence installed for the dogs. We can only leave them on a lead in the front driveway during the day for so long. We find a guy in the yellow pages and phone him and he comes out and gives us a very attractive quote. He says he'll be there next Thursday to start digging the holes for the fence posts and that he'll want a 50% deposit to buy materials which isn't the best sign.

"Really?" we ask ourselves, a business that can't afford to buy materials? We say okay but we aren't too excited about this. Thursday comes and Mike calls him. No answer. Mike leaves a message. No response. A few days go by and Mike calls again. A few more days go by and we say, "screw it, let's find somebody else."

We find another coyote fence installer (that's what those rustic southwest fences made from cedar are called) and we're pretty happy because this guy actually lives in our community of Eldorado and he provides us with several references from people in our neighborhood. He's got the posts in and is hanging the new fence when we finally hear back from the first guy who is incredulous that we rolled with somebody else and gives us some sorry ass excuse about a niece and her car. Maybe we've got too much city in us, maybe we just need to slow down the pace, but we're smug that someone who would have probably stretched the job out for a very long time didn't dupe us.

Wilma acclimates to the snow

With the fence up the dogs now have a nice sized space to play and explore. They learn new games like find the ball in the snow and let's howl with the coyotes at night.

I worry about them in the cold so we bring them into the garage where the slab outside of the door from the garage into the house is heated and they are out of the wind at night or when the day is particularly bitter. I spend $150 and order two heated whelping pads for their outdoor doghouses and an electric dog bowl that will keep their water from freezing. The whelping pads arrive on a day when we have another contractor in the house doing some odd jobs including attempting to fix some broken floor tiles. As he pulls each tile up he simultaneously cracks the adjacent two or three tiles in a spider's web pattern, and on we go tile by tile so that the small cracked tile issue is now a big cracked tile issue. I finally tell him to stop since there doesn't seem to be a good solution to fix these hairline fractures we'll just live with them, that's what rugs are for.

With the new heated pads plugged in and nicely toasting up the doghouses I go out to check on the dogs and find that Pancho clearly did not like this invader in his hut and he has decided to bite the pad's electric cord in half—déjà vu to Malibu lights. How he managed to do this and not get totally electrocuted remains a mystery. My *keep them warm* solution has lasted for a whole hour and I pull the other pad sensing he'll do that same to that one. At least the water bowl remains undisturbed, intact and will serve both the dogs during the rest of their lives and later the wild birds too.

This type of mañana time we experienced with the first fence guy continues with a variety of contractors we deal with over the years, some worse than others. From the plumber who was to order a part and several months later when I call to follow up says, "Oh, did you still want that?" to the flooring guy who tells us he can't install the laminate wood flooring we bought after we've ripped up and disposed of all our old carpeting because the floor now will not accept this product, to the kitchen counter guys my husband has to cajole to arrive on time and get the job done, actually going so far as to pose as a supplier to get their direct number from the big box store who sold us the upgrade so we can make sure they are coming to our jobsite each day. There is certainly the reason the state still has the word "Mexico" in the name. Oh si!

Fifteen

Stupid Jobs

We haven't been in Santa Fe for more than a month when we decide it is time that we find work to pay for daily essentials and things like our medical, car and home insurance. Naively we think we can just get menial jobs and they will sustain our lifestyle into the infinite future since we no longer have a mortgage. Our attitudes are, "hey, what is there to worry about?" Mike finds a job in town at an office supply store and I get one next door to him at a pharmacy. Things are going well. We still don't know anyone here yet *really* but we've done the initial improvements and changes we wanted to on the house, we've seen many of the local Santa Fe sights and have gone out to eat quite a bit (something we rarely did in Valley Center). Our coworkers are nice enough and we're acclimating to our town, the altitude, and the winter weather.

We've been at our jobs for three or four weeks when Mike appears one afternoon at the pharmacy window to tell me it is snowing really hard outside and that I should leave work now so I can follow him home. I'm thinking that I am new here, and I don't leave work early and Mike is probably overreacting. I mean, how much snow could it really be? My boss, a super nice man and the head pharmacist tells me it would be wise to listen to Mike and go. I walk outside and I cannot believe how much snow there is. It is halfway up my tires and I can't even see my car, only her shape. I use my gloves to scrape the snow off and as soon as I have navigated a circle around the car extracting snow, it is completely covered again. Meanwhile I can no longer feel my fingers as the cold has bitten through my gloves leaving my hands red and numb. I decide then and there I need an ice scraper.

We pull out of the lot, my bug behind Mike's truck and we head towards the freeway onramp for the 25 North towards

Denver and the infamous Raton Pass—heading in the direction of Eldorado. The highway patrol has shut down the freeway onramp telling us it isn't safe to pass—its roughly 4:30 in the afternoon but the sky has grown dark and the clouds are angry. We're thinking what the heck do we do now, we have our dogs outside in this stuff and we want to get home. We learn that our home, just east of town, is where the road is normally closed when there is a heavy snowstorm. Mike decides we'll take the Old Las Vegas highway, a small narrow little road that was there before the freeway came in. It takes us several u-turns to figure out where we are, and then two hours of driving at a snail's pace until we arrive at our house—a mere 12 miles from work. It's the same story as our drive to Santa Fe from San Diego. I'm terrified and humming at the top of my lungs to calm myself as I follow Mike's truck in the darkness home. We're cold and hungry, as are the dogs, but we arrive home and we're all safe and that is the important thing.

The snow continues to fall heavy all night and while Mike goes into work via his truck the next morning, my Volkswagon is too low to navigate the roads. We're on different work schedules so I call my boss Mark and he is very understanding.

All told we get four feet of snow and it is bloody cold. Our back patio is an ice floe and we risk our lives taking the dogs out on walks around the neighborhood on the frozen pavement. Despite being 7,000 feet high the town doesn't have the capacity, planning or equipment to effectively clear the roads of snow in a timely fashion. We go nearly a week without mail delivery and three weeks for trash collection, as our road is just too full of snow for these vehicles to safely pass. Good thing we have lots of canned dog food and groceries.

*****

Snow, snow, and more freaking snow!

Four feet of the white stuff

The first of many days Mike threatens to return to sunny San Diego

By late spring Mike and I have decided that our "stupid jobs" aren't the right fit. Mike moves on to work for a bank for a short stint, and I accept a position to do purchasing for a jewelry company. Our offices are close and we often meet for lunch at a rose garden in town to picnic on the grass—not something we were ever able to do in San Diego. It's a lovely park, usually with a crowd of Tai Chi'ers practicing and the enticing aroma and sight of a hundred different colors of rose bushes. It is exciting to watch the snow dwindle and the first signs of spring hit dormant bushes and trees. By May there is an explosion of forsythia and lilacs, and the hollyhocks start making their appearance in every yard, and fill the cracks of the city sidewalks like weeds.

The sun is out and the lilacs are blooming

We start to make some friendships finally. I've got some nice coworkers at the jewelry company and we've started to meet a few more neighbors. I've joined a yoga and fitness studio in Eldorado and can call at least twenty ladies who exercise there my friends. In town we begin to recognize more people and laugh when someone tells us, "New Mexico is a small town."

*****

We get a number of San Diego and Vermont visitors to our home throughout this first full year in Santa Fe so we're kept busy with entertaining and showing people the New Mexico sites like the downtown Santa Fe Plaza, Harry's Diner, Canyon Road, Museum Hill, Abiquiu, Taos, the Rio Grande Gorge, Los Alamos, plus all the festivals and music events. Since it is all just as new to us too we enjoy it and won't take a real vacation until later next year.

In June the monsoon season starts, and the summer, which follows a very windy spring, isn't what we would call mild either. Impressive, but terrifying for Wilma, the thunder and lightening roll in with a vengeance and for several hours each afternoon wreak havoc on her senses and consequently on our property too.

We find that over the course of the summer Wilma has chewed the doorjambs and handle on the door into the garage, badly scratched the stucco, dug up the utilities to the phone *again*, causing us to contract to have the fence moved to make this area non-accessible to her, destroyed several plants and chewed our garden hose in half, *twice*. Thus begins our ongoing trips to the vet with Wilma to repair teeth she has cracked by chewing metal chains and fences and to get her a continuous supply of acepromazine in an effort to quell her anxiety.

Our anxiety goes up too as we know every time a storm passes, which is daily in the summer, Wilma is going to go ballistic and who knows what the outcome will be. We have flash backs to Betty's unacceptable behavior and know it runs in the genes, another skitzo dog. Pancho meanwhile is totally nonplussed by the storms.

Mike and I find the storms fascinating—horrendous displays of light, sound, and moisture that have us diving to close windows and the front door as they build and release. The storm clouds literally form, brew and gain steam over the Sangre de Cristo Mountains directly outside our backdoor. Our immediate neighbors Rick and Letty tell us that they've gone through several microwave ovens that have been obliterated by the electric strikes so Mike and I put every appliance on a circuit breaker and either turn the entire panels off when not in use or unplug things we aren't using. Meanwhile I don't bother the new flagpole I've had Mike erect in the backyard. I let my various flags fly, rain or shine, so I don't end up getting myself electrocuted.

Mike makes another job change in late summer. He now works for a medical supply sales company and drives a van full of bandages, aspirin, and safety supplies around to existing and potential customers. When he drives out to the more remote Indian Reservations they always say, "Hey, the medicine man is here." A phrase that always causes us gringos laugh at the irony.

This new job takes Mike all over northern New Mexico. He starts seeing beautiful areas that we then go back to later on weekends to hike at or picnic. It also exposes him to the extreme poverty that lies outside of Santa Fe in rusted trailers and dilapidated homes. Mike will keep this job for the duration of our time in Santa Fe and tells me often that it has taught him some good life lessons such as taking people for who they are and not judging by appearances. He has customers in the middle of nowhere that look poor and unkempt and spend $1500, paying him in full and they've never even met him before, and he has swanky-rich Santa Fe hotels go into collections over unpaid bills. He befriends tattoo artists who marvel at the canvas of his untouched skin while they've little if any left themselves, and plenty of self-made business men and women who come from humble beginnings and treat him like part of their families. Mike's friendships with these business owners swells and when I get bumped on the freeway onramp by an inattentive young lady we get a deal on auto-body work, not to mention the many reduced-priced New Mexican restaurant meals.

Sixteen

The Economic Crisis of 2006-2007

In May of 2006 I give my notice at the jewelry company. I've worked there for a year but I am bored and uninspired. For the first time in my life I am going to take a break from working. I've manage to save some cash and my dad has given me some money too so I decide to take the rest of the year off and do some improvements on our home and just enjoy life without working. I do yard work and painting. Mike is out of town once or twice a month on overnighters so I use those times to knock out painting a couple of rooms at a time. I have a blast taping a sawtooth cutout design around some of the doorways—something I saw at a bed and breakfast in Taos—and painting bright and contrasting colors then watching his reaction upon returning home. Our kitchen becomes red and black, our bedroom blue and tan, and I use turquoise and rich brown in the master bathroom. The rest of the house gets a coat of Tuscan clay sand paint, and our oversized southwest desert scene painting hung in the living room is set off by the interesting swirling texture and hue. I like the finished product, as does Mike who used to only want white and bright in our former homes.

Our teeny tiny living room in Santa Fe

The kitchen is completely redone in red and black

Lots of painting went on this year and no room was spared

Of course when you paint, then you have to buy complimentary light switch plate covers, cabinet knobs, towels and linens, throw pillows and so on, so what starts as a few cans of paint and some elbow grease and time becomes several thousand dollars spent later. Next comes some new appliances, a quartz countertop in the kitchen, an improvement in the guest bathroom and new flooring. Over time we'll end up having the house re-stuccoed, new windows installed, and gravel brought in for the driveway and the dog run, and so much more.

In the vein of trying to make improvements that will save us money we have a water diversion added to our washing machine so we can reuse the gray water to nourish thirsty plants. We literally have a valve we can turn to bypass the rinse water from the machine into a 55 gallon drum and we then move the water by hand in two gallon buckets. It was only after a few years that Mike figures out we could run a hose from the bucket to some of the trees to water them and save our backs and shoulders.

I decide I want a clothesline to dry our clothes on during the hot summers and save the energy used from running the dryer. So at first I string some old speaker wire across the fenced area where the dogs are but determine it is too low as Wilma has taken to walking through and under the wet, clean clothes. To fix that scenario I buy a circular clothesline online from Ireland of all places. Mike cements it into the fenced area

110

but this time the line was out of the dog's reach, but still hidden from passersby.

The new foam roof we have installed lowers our heating bill as it keeps things toasty in the winter and cool in the summer. We also have the boiler updated, and the skylights resealed. And the double paned windows also add to the insulation making our electric bills drop to around $30 in the summer—a far cry from the $160 we were paying in Valley Center.

I buy two circular composting bins and every bit of compostable food scrap, coffee grinds, paper product and even dryer lint goes into the bin. It freezes in the winter, but we continue to add to it. In the spring after it thaws and cooks everything I use it to fertilize my outdoor plants.

During my time off I not only update the house and play in the yard, but I find time for lots of exercise, and spending time with the dogs, old Mahalo and our newest buddy, Billy the Kid, a seven year-old mackerel-colored tabby cat that we've adopted from a bad smelling shelter in Española.

My dad comes out to visit while I'm on hiatus and it is wonderful. One of the first times in years we've spent that much one-to-one time. I notice my dad seems very distracted and unsteady since the last time I saw him. I take him for a short walk along Canyon Road and he has some troubles, he falls when we visit the Audubon Center. He is distracted at a wine festival we take him to—and my dad *loves* wine. After he returns home and goes through a series of tests, we realize he has the beginning stages of Alzheimer's and this fact will have a profound influence on some of our future plans and decisions, though at the time I guiltily admit I felt irritated at what seems to be his unwillingness to stay focused and present-centered.

My dad and I at a wine festival in Santa Fe

Dad at Pecos National Historical Park

Late in the summer we go out of town to the Telluride Blues and Brews festival in Colorado. Our neighbor Letty, who has a pet care business, is hired to take care of all our beasts. It's wonderful to get away for a short driving trip and we have a fabulous time staying in Ouray, soaking in the mineral hot springs, and then partaking in the wonderful food, beer and music festival in scenic Telluride.

One of Mike's grandmothers passes this year and leaves him $10,000. He tells me he will do what his grandparents, who were worldly folks, would have wanted—save $5,000 and take me on a Mexican Riviera cruise with the rest. So in October when the weather begins to turn cool in New Mexico, we go on a glorious eleven-day trip to Cabo San Lucas, Loreto, La Paz, Mazatlan, Puerta Vallarta, and Acapulco. We've always really enjoyed Mexico and love the coastal seaside towns, so full of colors, delicious food, music, and laughter. While exploring each south-of-the-border city our adventurous side gets to simmering and we actually discuss the possibility of moving to Mexico at some point for an early retirement. "How much different could it be from New Mexico anyways?" Mike says.

Beers in Cabo

The ship disembarks in San Diego when we return so we take the time to visit with family while we are there for a couple of days. I think I wanted to leave San Diego so badly a few years ago that I don't even miss the place on this visit, regardless of family ties and amazing weather, but that will all change soon enough.

Back in Santa Fe we enjoy the last of the cool evenings and the smell of roasting green chiles and then buckle down for another winter.

*****

With dwindling funds, I begin looking for employment in December. I interview in the middle of the holidays and land a position with a non-profit called Forest Guardians in Santa Fe as their Office Manager. I start work later in January and thus begins my career as a paid treehugger. I'm back to commuting into town, in the snow, which I don't like, so I jump at the opportunity to take public transportation that is offered for a mere $1.00 each way. I drive the three miles to where the bus picks up in the winter near our home and then have to walk about a half mile to my office where it drops me off in town. I feel like this is another step in simplification and I like it. Mike however isn't loving the snow since he has to essentially work in it every day while I stay semi-warm in the Forest Guardians' office downtown. One morning I see him marching back to the house before I leave for work with the door handle to his van in his hand. It was so bloody cold the thing froze and broke off when he tried to open the sliding door to access his product inside. He lets me know in no uncertain terms that he really does not like the cold or winter, nor Santa Fe at that particular moment.

*****

In the fall we take a ten-day trip we've been planning for a year to France and Belgium with my aunt Cheryl and her husband Kyle. It's lovely, though not super warm. I spend a lot of money on clothes before we leave that I don't really need—but I feel so stylish and Parisian in them so I splurge, I simply must have these clothes—most of which I'll never wear again and practically give away at a designer resale shop. I've spent months looking at fashion magazines because I feel so deprived living in Santa Fe where most folks wear sweats so the fact that I can glam it up is super exciting to me. I concentrate on what hairstyle to get, what jewelry to wear, even what make-up to buy. I end up spending several thousand dollars and actually have a credit card bill again. Looking back, this trip now lives on the precipice of so many things that are just not that important to me—the image, the trappings, and the lavish accessories.

Mike and I in Luxembourg Gardens, Paris, France

L'Orange, France

Now that is a beer en France

2007 represents the kick-off of the latest fiscal crisis; one we really start to feel in 2008 despite being mortgage free.

Seventeen

The Living Wage

When we selected Santa Fe as a place to relocate to and live mortgage free we looked at the location, weather, crime, ambiance, etc., most of which appealed to us, some we chose to overlook, some which was misrepresented (hello four feet of snow and crooked sheriff) and some unknown and non-existent at the time.

Being at 7,000 feet and a little out of the way, almost all of the food and beverages are trucked in during the winter, although in the summer there is a plethora of produce, breads, eggs and cheeses from the local farming communities, and it is of both photogenic quality and mighty tasty. There isn't a lot of competition for most commodities and services in general so in many cases one or two businesses monopolize the market and you are simply stuck. Unless you want to drive an hour to the big city of Albuquerque, you have to pay the current price or go without. I was astonished that a simple haircut for women commands $70 in Santa Fe, and that a service like a haircut is taxed. So a trim ends up costing a whopping $90 after you add in the tip. Tomatoes and alcohol—wine and beer—are also much more expensive than I was accustomed to paying in San Diego. I have to pay up to $5 for a single, organic tomato and a six-pack of beer is $12. Trader Joe's "two buck chuck" is more like "four buck chuck" in Santa Fe.

So in 2008, as the economic crisis gets underway, our wages stayed flat and the cost of goods and services skyrocket in comparison. To make matters even more challenging, Santa Fe's living wage also starts to creep up causing business owners who don't shutter their doors to pass on those costs to the public. From 2004 until 2013 the minimum wage goes from $8.50 an hour to $10.66, but the service and the quality of those workers remains the same—in general, not that great. We have now gone from the kind of grocery shopping of "throw what you want into the shopping cart" to "where can I get the best deal on such-and-such." We look for value, not that we didn't care before, but now it has become essential if we want to minimize our expenditures. The fact that we don't have a mortgage is a godsend, we often ask ourselves what we'd do if we had to pay a mortgage and it would mean that we would never get out of Dodge. Despite the start of the fiscal meltdown we still manage to go to Playa Del Carmen during the winter, then we take a week long driving trip throughout Colorado during the summer and a brief trip to San Diego for my dad's 75th birthday in August.

On our San Diego trip Mike starts talking about wanting to go back. I'm thinking sure, sounds fun and I miss my family and worry about my dad, but we've got a lot of animals and I have no desire to get back into the daily grind of working to support stuff again. I tell him that he'd have to do that too, push himself really hard for the mighty dollar and that doesn't sound too good to him either. But, Mike being Mike, the dreamer and planner, starts to spend a lot of time researching condominiums in downtown San Diego. He familiarizes himself with the various builders, construction types—cement is better than stick built—and average costs. He continues to show me these condos, and their plummeting asking prices, and over the course of another cold and snowy winter we start to fantasize what it would be like to live in urban, downtown San Diego. Somehow we have gotten ourselves thinking about acquiring things again, ultra modern furniture, sumptuous furnishings, and taking on an expensive monthly fee that will continue to rise into perpetuity for one of these downtown high rises. We fanaticize about walking to cafes, along the harbor, living urban. It all sounds thrilling and we both feel invigorated and entertain taking on a new fast-paced lifestyle, one of those what-the-heck are we thinking scenarios that we've played out before and will again.

In February of 2009 we head for Mexico again to get out of the freezing Rocky Mountains—fortunately Mexico is really inexpensive travel from the southwest and Mike spends a lot of time looking for the best value. This time we choose Puerto Vallarta for our vacation. We love the colors, the food, the warm weather, ocean and friendly people. We don't like how touristy this city is—the constant barrage of people wanting you to buy their trinkets—nor being burglarized in the middle of the night while we sleep—a story for another time, but still, Mike has an epiphany on this trip, what if we moved to Mexico, or somewhere internationally where we could stretch our money instead of San Diego? At that moment, as we looked at the economy in 2009 we both realize that this seems like a better option than a depressed market in San Diego. Who are we fooling thinking we'll get high-paying jobs and a flashy apartment during a financial meltdown? Everybody is looking for a job and irrespective of contacts we have in my hometown the chances of us landing high-paying positions to support a pricy condo really isn't realistic.

Eighteen

Mexico Bound

I guess we are both born risk takers and aren't the stay-in-your-hometown-and-never-leave status quo type. We love adventure and are willing to roll the dice on something fresh, new, and different. We love change and challenge. Mike subscribes to a number of travel and relocation magazines geared toward expatriates. He always becomes very focused with any kind of planning, a real strength, and so he starts to learn what cities in Mexico are the safest, the best value, the most history, which have better climate. He learns about so many coastal communities that I get dizzy from all the information he manages to push my way.

First, there is San Miguel de Allende, a city touted to be both quaint and cosmopolitan and once an important stop on the silver route. More than one book and documentary has been made to highlight how romantic and artsy, and friendly to westerners including Americans, Canadians and Europeans this city has become. Mike devours all he can on this place and shares every morsel.

Then there is Guanajuato. Also a silver town, Guanajuato is a UNESCO World Heritage Site and a charming colonial-era city situated in a picturesque valley. The super cool thing about this city is the underground network of tunnels runs beneath the city helping to control the flow of traffic. Like San Miguel, it is artsy, clean and safe for expats.

Thirdly, Mike looks at Mazatlan. Miles of sandy beaches along the Pacific coast, Mazatlan is American friendly with sunshine, seafood, beer—*hello Pacifico*—and plenty to do.

We have a six-mile walk we do a few times a week in our Eldorado neighborhood and we practice the Spanish we've been learning on the computer and in books while we walk and dream about what life *could be like* on pennies a day. It's fun to learn. We purchase an easy-to-learn Spanish book that contains flashcards with of names of fruits, furniture, rooms, etc. and we stick these all over the house to mindfully challenge ourselves to learn the language. Before long we are talking about manzanas and queso, the tabla and silla, and the dormitorio and baño with ease.

Mike looks at apartment rentals in Mazatlan and other locales and shares what he finds online with me. One bedroom, a bath, kitchen and sitting room apartments rent for under $500 a month. We consider what we would want to keep and move, would we want to drive a car down there or buy one when we arrive, or do we even need a car? What are the taxes, immigration laws, and income requirements for non-residents? Ironically while we fight here domestically in the states over Mexican immigration rights and pay for medical expenses for lots of immigrant families, in Mexico you have to show a certain fixed income or savings in order to stay in their country so that you are not a financial or social burden—it showed us that American politicians have a lot of learning to do and could do so by copying, not opposing, our neighbors to the south.

We know leaving is a ways off and we're both still checked into our home so in an effort to still enjoy it while we are there we undertake a few more improvements. We decide to get a new bathroom sink with molded countertop and replace the carpet with pet-friendly hardwood floors. Both endeavors become fiascos. Let's just say that the handyman/plumber we hire for the sink is a very sloppy worker and in the end Mike could have done a better installation. The flooring is another story entirely.

Just two months after the Puerto Vallarta nighttime robbery, our home is burglarized too. I come home one afternoon to find our front door kicked in, stereo equipment queued by the front door, computers, a rifle, and jewelry all missing. I can tell that the thieves include a woman, or otherwise meticulous person, because the jewelry has been hand-selected out of my jewelry trays, something a guy would never do and would opt to just dump the entire contents into a pillowcase. Our neighbors tell us Wilma and Pancho were going particularly nuts barking that day but they thought it was just a coyote and so they didn't pay much attention. Thankfully neither the burglars, nor the coyotes, hurt the cats and while Billy has the opportunity to roam outside, old Mahalo just snoozes safely on the bed strewn between drawers and half-emptied jewelry containers. I'm beside myself when I get home and see that someone has combed through our belongings in search of quick-to-sell items for drug money. I'm pissed and wish I could have caught them in the act—I would have certainly strangled them all.

*****

Even though our home is small we still have two dogs and two cats and I am just so tired of all the responsibilities. Taking care of animals, a yard, a three bedroom home, and working full time is making me feel frazzled so cashing out and moving somewhere that we can afford is intoxicating to me.

We visit family in Vermont again this year, certain that this will be one of our last trips to the East Coast. We begin to prepare family for our eventual move south and everyone really seems on board. They get it when we talk about what it takes to retire today and how far our money could go in another country.

I end up getting furloughed every other Friday due to the tough economy and though I love the extra time off, I feel it in the wallet. We create spreadsheet after spreadsheet on costs, scenarios and money needs to make this move happen. We have different target dates depending on how our savings grows which ends up not being a lot, savings returns have been squashed flat and just lie there unmoving at under 1%.

In anticipation of moving to Mexico or Central America we start slowly unloading our "stuff." We host garage sale after garage sale—first with our neighbors and then more frequently on our own. It is shocking to see how much time and effort goes into selecting things you want to own and then how little you get back if you can actually entice someone to buy it— there is truth in the phrase pennies on the dollar. From compact discs, art, linens, furniture, books, electronics and infinite supplies of doodads, we move our inventory slowly...hauling stuff outside into the garage, pricing each item, posting signs everywhere, advertising in the paper. Then, the people show up early, often before you've even opened up the garage to get the best pickings. Not a garage sale aficionado myself, I never knew there was such an art to the entire process. People actually comb the paper for where garage sales are happening and then route a map, hitting random ones unadvertised in the middle of their course. The ones that really know what they are doing get there first and look for high quality items they can lowball and then plan to sell themselves on EBay or other ways. In the beginning our sales last two days, meaning there goes your entire weekend just sitting and waiting for people to come up the road—plus I naively think that renting tables to better display the small items is a great idea and spend an outrageous amount to pick up five long beaten-up tables from a party supply place and afterwards redeliver them. Later in the process we just do single day sales and then even further in this multi-year process we resort to simply bringing a lot of our "stuff" to the animal shelter donation store so they can sell everything and reap the money. This business of unloading belongings is bittersweet. Bitter to part with autographed books, trinkets that meant something, furnishings we've enjoyed. But sweet too in the sense of cleaning house, paring belongings down to what really matters, getting clear to what, if any, of this "stuff" matters at all.

Next to the garage sales, Craigslist online and posting small sale signs at the local grocery store bulletin board is the next best thing. We have infinite stories of Craigslist customers—many, fantastic people who come out to buy our BBQ, wine-making materials, compost bins, bikes, satellite dish, tools and ladders, strained glass equipment, televisions, paintings, horse troughs used for growing produce, and a plethora of other items. Some were strange encounters, people making appointments and never showing up, or keeping us around all afternoon waiting for them only to have them show up, love the item, and then tell us, "Sorry, I just don't have the dough right now to make a purchase."

My favorite however was an artist and his wife who came in towards the end and bought our entire bedroom set, and all our back patio furniture, and then proceeded to inquire about items still hanging on our walls, asking if they could buy this or that. In the end this was fantastic, yielding us nearly $3,000 and had us sleeping on a lumpy futon the last six months we remained in Santa Fe.

The next several years we will unload a substantial amount of stuff and in the end we realize we don't miss much.

*****

Another Christmas comes and goes, a few packages arrive in the mail with "stuff" in them and we both groan. We make a pact then and there with many relatives to just skip the entire gift exchange and keep it to consumables if they must. We manage to go to Ten Thousand Waves near that Santa Fe Ski Area for a couple's massage and soak on Christmas Eve, followed by dinner near the Plaza. We luck out and we're able to get pizza and a salad to share at half price. We're appreciative for the deal.

Old Mahalo is fast approaching his 21st year. It's early February 2010 and surprising a little temperate outside for this time of year. This old cat is nothing but a bag of bones, but he still manages to eat—especially treats—and has a personality bigger than life. Because the weather for this winter is mild in comparison to many others, he still wants to go sit outside in the front courtyard next to the wall where warmth radiates. He hasn't tried to scale the courtyard wall since he was about 16 so I'm comfortable with him going out there, but I do keep a wary eye out for both avian and ground predators. In mid-February though I can tell it is time. He is so bony and his breath smells like death. He comes staggering in towards us one morning looking bewildered and near death. I tell Mike, "it's time" and he agrees. I carry the old boy to our vet's office after phoning them and they have a room ready. Mahalo goes very peacefully in my arms, the room has a cage of birds and they are tweeting. Life goes on despite our pain and loss. We loved that old cat.

Mahalo as an old kitty in the courtyard in Santa Fe

Rest in Peace Mahalo

In late April I leave to attend a Women's Writer's Workshop in South Carolina for a week. It's been a dream of mine for years to immerse myself in writing so I fly out on a Sunday and will be back the following Saturday. The trip is amazing and I get to meet, and bond with these inspiring women from all over the country and spend seven glorious days just writing, relaxing, sharing, reading, and walking all over the balmy island I am staying on called Seabrook Island. Mike and I Skype each other several times while I am gone. While I enjoy myself and learn my craft, Mike is freezing with an unexpected snowstorm. He shows me the snow falling as I giggle from the mess haul having a meal while the sun glistens.

When I return from the trip Mike has even more ideas about how we can "retire" within the next couple of years, but now he is looking at Ecuador instead of Mexico which offers even more for the U.S. dollar and he has done all kinds of calculations. "If we were to sell our home for xyz and take some of our retirement savings early well then we'll be set," he explains.

And just like that our trajectory has changed and we are learning about Quito, and Cuenca, and San Mateo Beach. How the locals wash clothes and sadly how guinea pigs are a dietary staple. We are reading more books, watching more documentaries, talking to knowledgeable people who have lived there.

*****

In July we are gearing up to go back to San Diego for another visit with family. We are deep in the midst of monsoon season again and Wilma, who is now eleven, is aged and filled with utter anxiety. She shakes with fervor when the thunderstorms start to brew and she tears at the house and herself in despair. We visit the vet frequently and they up her medications in an effort to keep her sedated and calm. The doses seem to have the opposite effect and Wilma is out of control. We really don't know what to do. We are worried she is going to have a heart attack. In a decision that is extremely difficult to make, and one I often wish I could take back, we decide to put her out of her psychological misery and put her down. It's difficult and terrible and regretful. But she is in a place where storms can no longer reach her and we don't all live in constant fear and pain. We will always cherish her memory.

Rest in Peace Wilma

Nineteen

Dang, It's Cold!

We've been living in Santa Fe for seven years now and as we move from 2010 to 2011 we have a horrific winter. It is bitterly cold, getting down to negative digits for nearly a week. Communities in Northern New Mexico actually lose power to heat their homes and there is suffering and illness as a result. Older people lose fingers and toes, as their trailers are too cold to keep them adequately protected. We are fortunate to be spared and are grateful we have ample food and warmth.

Pancho is the sole dog now and we spend lots of time with him. During this terrible cold front we bring him in with us, it is just too frigid for any creature to be exposed to the elements. With our radiant heat coming up from the floor Pancho is miserable and thus ensues going in and out, and in and out, hour upon hour to cool himself in the snow. Even crashing on the elevated couch on his blankie proves to be too warm for him.

We notice Pancho's hindquarters becoming more compromised. He has always baulked at having us touch his rear legs and now they have become more and more wobbly. When we take him for walks he starts sitting down to rest more frequently. Finally he cannot even make it to the corner of our street without resting. We bring him in to our vet after the cold front passes to find out what we might be able to do for him. Should we anticipate purchasing him a doggy wheel chair? The vet tells us that our problems are much larger than his hindquarters. As he puts his hands across Pancho's neck he can feel lots of tumors. Pancho has very advanced lymphoma cancer and the vet suggests we go through a series of procedures to extend Pancho's life for *several months*. We are heartbroken. We have just lost Mahalo and Wilma last year, and now Pancho is entering a phase where he will endure deep suffering. Again, we have to make a very difficult decision.

Pancho is euthanized on Valentine's Day 2011. We are both with him, as we have been with our other pets, stroking his fur, telling him we love him, telling him it will be okay, telling him goodbye. We both ball our eyes out. We weren't at all ready for something like this and it hurts so much. Always gentle, always a special boy. He will forever live on in our hearts.

Rest in Peace Pancho

Since winter is so long and often brutally cold, Mike books us another cruise this winter for the Caribbean. Letty takes care of our one remaining pet, Billy the cat, while Mike and I take off for warmer weather. We visit St. Thomas, Puerto Rico and Grand Turk. We snorkel, eat, drink, sun ourselves, walk, and have a very nice time. Our camera dies early on and we have little photos by which to remember this trip, just our memories and travel journal.

Twenty

A Thanksgiving to Remember

Like the former several years, this year too we continue with the garage sales. We're determined to retire young and move to some third world country south of the border so we can actually enjoy our time on this planet without it being a constant chasing of the dollar. We figure we have a few more years and we might as well be ready. We are hopeful that the real estate market will make some rebounds since the economic crisis started back in 2008 and the proceeds from our home will fund some of our living expenses. Our belongings shrink and we talk about minimalism, getting back to what we had when we first started out—a small apartment with the basics and a cat.

Meanwhile violence in some of these areas we entertained moving to has escalated and we hear more and more stories about shootings and expats returning, realizing that paradise has its drawbacks. Frankly I begin to wonder what the heck I am going to do with myself with all the extra time and the limitations I will have being fair and female in a Latin country.

While saving to eventually move, we continue to make time to travel. I'm turning fifty in 2012 and I've decided I want to go to Africa to celebrate. Being a 1960's kid I spent many a Sunday night watching Mutual of Omaha's Wild Kingdom and this is just something I have to do—visit Africa and go on a safari. I want to see the vast savannas, the lumbering giraffes, speedy impalas, majestic lions, and of course, the giants of the plains, the elephants. For months I plan this trip, reading books, travel websites, watching videos. I learn about the tour operators and speak with several in South Africa. Finally, I select a tour operator and the actual "camps" I want to visit, all started by a woman with a beautiful collection of resorts called Desert and

Delta. I book our trip for late May, which is their winter in the southern part of Africa.

In the meantime, we've scheduled a few short vacations for the fall. We want to spend time with Mike's sister before we consider moving away down south so we meet up in Austin, Texas for four days with Patty and Sam to relax, visit, take in some music and good food at a very cute bed and breakfast near the University. Mike's sister Patty leaves the arrangements to me and so I select a safari inspired room for Mike and I and a collegiate decorated room for Patty and Sam.

On the heels of this we head to San Diego for Thanksgiving. My father's Alzheimer's disease has progressed. He is forgetful, and beginning to have a more challenging time with communication. He also has the recent addition of a pacemaker because his heart was becoming so unstable. Mike's father is getting older also, although he is much more mobile and gets around town easily by walking or taking public transportation.

We end up staying with my dad and his wife Cheryle in Encinitas for the entire visit. We do lots of meals together and a great deal of sitting and talking. On Thanksgiving Day we drive down to the city to spend time with Mike's dad John. We go to the hotel where Mike first kissed me for an excellent champagne brunch. In between all of that, Mike and I find time to do daily walks along the ocean.

It's November mind you, and Santa Fe is already in the throes of another oncoming winter. I realize on this visit how much I miss my family and I suddenly remember all I love about being close to relatives, and I am thoroughly falling back in love with San Diego's lovely coast. Mike is feeling the same way.

It's the day after Thanksgiving and we're only "home" for a few more days. Mike says to me,

"You know Lori, if anything ever happened to you I'd come back here in a heartbeat."

"Seriously?"

"Seriously."

And it's settled as easily and quickly as that.

Twenty-one

Be Back in a Year

And so, there you have it. The Sunday after Thanksgiving we're sitting in my dad's back yard and Mike says,

"You know Don, Lori and I have been thinking a lot about this and we have decided that we're coming back."

"That's great!" My dad says and I wonder if he takes us seriously, if anyone will since we've been on this crazy quest to acquire, then move, then our talk about leaving the U.S. completely, first to various towns in Mexico, then Ecuador to becoming expats, and now we're going on about returning back to where we started.

"Once you leave, you can't come back," said that well-meaning relative when we left Valley Center for Santa Fe.

But it feels really right. It feels like we're on the path that makes the most sense to both of us, and so regardless of what we think others might think we decide we will be back in a year. Our target date is October 1st of 2012.

We probably could have flown back to New Mexico on our own exuberance rather than by airplane. Landing back in the land of enchantment we began to put our thoughts and plans into motion.

Mike shares that he thinks our trip to Africa might not be the best of timing since we have much to do but I disagree, plus I've already paid out the deposit and it's a lifelong dream for me.

"We're debt free right now Mike, we have no mortgage, no car payments, no credit card debt, now is the time to do this trip before we get back into the routine of paying rent, and possibly having to get a second car."

Mike cannot argue this one and being supportive concedes.

The next six months leading up to Africa consist of creating flyers to sale much of our furniture, meeting with and hiring a property manager to handle the rental of our property until the timing is better to sale, talking to our employers about the idea of allowing us to transfer—meaning I'll work virtually—and getting a vast array of vaccines for our trip. With our well-orchestrated plan we're able to accomplish all four things before we depart for South Africa.

We arrive in Johannesburg the last week of May and we have an utterly marvelous and flawlessly organized trip. Every detail of our entire vacation in Botswana and Zambia exceeds our expectations again and again. We take safari's daily, twice a day actually and every third day we get on a small plane and fly to another location. We see spellbinding wildlife—leopards, lions, wild dogs, zebras and tons of elephants. We have freshly prepared meals, are entertained by African singing, cocktail hours with spectacular drinks and conversations and views, and meet other exciting travelers from all over the world. I realize even now looking back how much I felt *in the moment* in Africa; how genuine each and every person I met was; how the experience of something so profound has more meaning to me than anything I could ever buy and own.

Two bulls at Makgadikgadi Pans National Park, Botswana

133

Mike and I having a sundowner drink out in the African wild

Zebras, zebras everywhere

The flying banana, these birds are everywhere in Botswana

I don't need drugs to get high because life does that for me. I relive so much of the trip when I get back that sleeping on a futon that we had in a back bedroom for our occasional guests doesn't even phase me. Our nightstands are cardboard boxes. All but one of our lamps is sold so we have to move the final one about to provide extra light for reading and we resort to flashlights in our bedroom.

We're back from Africa for just a few weeks and then we're off again, this time to visit family in Vermont. Mike's grandmother is turning 100 and the entire extended family is going. At first Mike was a bit hesitant about the trip. We've just returned from the most expensive trip we'll probably ever take in our lifetime, and now I'm encouraging him to spend more money for a trip to the East coast. But I can see it for what it is. It's another opportunity of a lifetime and I know we'd both kick ourselves if we missed this.

The weather when we arrive late June in Vermont is splendid, if not a little on the warm side. The trip is a whirlwind of family, beautifully prepared foods, tons of photographs, free flowing wine, family, hugs and love. Mim, Mike's grandmother, is utterly moved by all the family and Mike and I have such a great time sitting on the back deck of Aunt Peggy and Uncle Bob's home. Mike connects with cousins he hadn't seen in years and I get to meet some I'd never met before. This is the kind of family gathering everyone should be so blessed to have. Again, this type of interaction with others is so much more meaningful to us than belongings, and continues to cement the kind of life we choose to live.

Mike and I with his lovely Grandmother on her 100ᵗʰ birthday

Mike's relatives are excited to hear our news of our plan to return to San Diego, and there unfolds even some remote and distant plans for one of Mike's cousins to come out and stay at our place in the future.

*****

We're down to our final four months now in Santa Fe. We continue to host a few more garage sales and then finally just bring the remaining stuff to the Humane Society's store so they can sell what's left for profit. During one of the garage sales Mike overhears a woman talking about wanting to rent in Eldorado because she works at the hospital nearby but lives several hours north. Mike is in sales for a living so his ears perk right up—he has salesman radar. He gives Denise the grand tour of our place, even getting her to sit in one of our Adirondack chairs out back so she can view the wildlife flocking at our bird feeders and see the flowers and view. She loves our place so we immediately contact the property management company we've interviewed to handle our property and within a week we've got a contract to rent out our place in the fall.

Life gets into overdrive now but we remain grounded. I'm determined to enjoy each and every final moment in our little pueblo style home and relish the wildlife, beautiful Sangre de Cristo vistas, and the dramatic monsoon storms that sweep through during the summer.

Coyotes outside our back door in Santa Fe

A family of scaled quail in at our birdbath

Appreciating all of the wildlife, even the bunnies

Part of my grounding also includes a personal commitment I made to myself for my 50th year: to run a half marathon. For most of the time during our eight years in Santa Fe we cycled, I took various fitness classes and yoga, and did a bit of jogging now and then. I think 50 is the year you kind of say to yourself, "wow, I'm getting older, but just how quickly do I intend to let myself age?" As I pondered that I sign up for a half in Albuquerque to happen in the middle of September, knowing we want to be moved out before the first of October then I get to running.

It's funny how neighbors seeing you running can start a conversation. We've already grown friendly with our immediate neighbors, hosting annual parties and being invited to theirs. Now I see them more often, early in the morning or midday on a weekend and it provides more conversation. They are encouraging which makes me happy and wanting to run even harder. I want to do this and I will.

Down to our remaining month in Santa Fe we drive out to San Diego over Labor Day weekend to check out and secure an apartment. We've already decided we don't want to buy a home and go into debt right now, but instead, would rather rent and then reconsider our options after we sale our Santa Fe home in the future. Mike has already lined up several apartments he has checked out on the internet that are west of the I-5 in Carlsbad and will accept kitties.

When we decided to move back I told Mike I would live anywhere he chose, as long as it was west of the I-5, which means coastal. He'd become very unhappy in Santa Fe, especially during winter when it was frigid and snowy so I felt like I owed that to him to choose the coastal town he wanted. He's always loved Carlsbad so I was game.

As we drive straight into San Diego we go immediately to the number one choice on his list. We meet with a woman in her late 70's named Betty who is clearly a chain smoker, firm in her attitude, but a complete peach of a person. She shows us the only available apartment in the complex, and though it doesn't meet all of our criteria we know it is a steal for the rent and sign the contract immediately. We tell her we can't move in for 30 days and she agrees to hold the place for us. We are ecstatic.

When we get to my dad's place, where we'll be staying and leaving our car so we can fly back and then move our stuff out the next month, he is so happy. It's thrilling. Mike is excited about getting back to a city he loves, and I am too. My dad is so proud and he and Cheryle and Mike and I go out for a nice dinner that evening to celebrate. My dad keeps say, "You two put your mind to it and you can accomplish anything." He is clearly impressed that we made a plan, executed each piece, and now we were heading into the home stretch.

We fly back home leaving our car and use Mike's truck for the rest of our stay in New Mexico. Mike decides that bringing his truck to San Diego isn't necessary since his employer has made a place for him to transfer to in San Diego and provides a company vehicle and mine has agreed to allow me to work virtually so we decide we can get by on one car. The day before my half marathon Mike brings the truck to a dealer in Albuquerque and they agree to take it at a certain price. It isn't an ideal price but it is a price we can live with for a hassle free transfer and eliminating the headache of trying to sell it ourselves. I run my race on Sunday morning and place second in my age group. We drive home on a cloud with plans to return the following weekend to sell his truck, rent a car and have a final week in Santa Fe before moving.

We're all packed the day before the movers show up. Mike has booked a moving van that we will drive but we have movers show up to load the truck. Mike has ordered a truck three times the size we actually need and the movers load our stuff with enough extra room for several pool tables. The van is parked in the driveway and we put Billy the Kid in the large doghouse outback where he'll be safe and head into town for a final meal. The cleaners arrive and further detail the house. The plan is we sleep on the floor tonight, get up early, leave with the rental car and moving van and eat breakfast at a restaurant next door to the auto rental return place and get out of dodge by 8:00am. Our renters are anxious to get in and are hoping to move in the night we sleep on the floor, but all works out as they prepare to arrive as we drive away.

Twenty-two

We're Back...Life at 360°

The move goes well, with Billy the Kid riding up front with us as we make our way across New Mexico, Arizona and to the California coast. It's bittersweet to know the pets we brought with us from San Diego rest on our property in Santa Fe, and the cat we adopted there now lives comfortably at the beach in sunny San Diego. Along the way across the desert I take Billy out of his crate and he lies comfortably in his cat bed, uncomplaining, while I stroke his head. It's as if he is thinking, "I'm good, as long as I am with you both."

The neon green shorts that Mike had when I first met him are long gone. But we both feel like we're back to where we started. We have no yard, no home maintenance, no debt, minimal belongings, only one furry companion, and a single car in one of America's most populated and beautiful cities.

Since returning much has happened, we've rekindled relationships with not just family here, but also friends—many who date back to our wedding and bow tie and mini-skirt party. We also joined a nearby yoga studio where we have found community. And we find ourselves with just as many friends our age and older as we do with people in their twenties, thirties and forties. It's an amazing collection of people who are fun-loving, giving, and easy going.

Another nice bonus to our location is the proximity not just to the ocean, but to the train station as well. With Mike's dad living downtown San Diego its an easy train ride down the coast for a visit. This works particularly well on the rare occasion when we'd both like to use the car to do separate things.

141

Mike and his dad John indulge in a beer

After two years our tenants in Santa Fe decide not to renew their lease and we decide to go ahead and sell our sweet little home. We both know we will take a pretty good loss because we bought at the top of the market and it has never recovered there. One very non-communicative realtor and lots of looky-loos and unreasonable offers later, we finally get an offer we can live with and absolve ourselves of the burdens of home ownership. It feels good to cut our losses and move on recognizing that though money does provide for a nice life, it isn't the end all, be all. It is interesting to us both how so many people will remain tied to a thing, person or location because they don't recognize that they have the option to walk away. They remain tied to what they paid for something and not factor in what their freedom is worth.

A few months after our home sells my father enters hospice and passes in early 2015. I am thankful that I've had the last several years back in San Diego to spend time with him and his wife Cheryle. His passing causes me to reflect even more on what makes up a good, well-lived life and what I want from mine. It reconfirms the desire for family and friendships over any material thing and that cutting burdens, debts and obligations can bring tremendous satisfaction.

My dad Don and his wife Cheryle on Christmas Day 2012

Now back and in our life of simplicity, we really wouldn't want it any other way. We're in a position where we could turn and accumulate again, own another home or condominium; drive a nicer, newer car but why? We've found our way, and it was right where we began. From here forward we're devoted to just keeping life casual and simple. It's nice to finally be back and have that all figured out with crystal clarity vision.

*****

Where we live, the apartment complex itself isn't perfect by any means. We don't have a team of unruly Italians living below us but we do hear doors slam, Mexican radios blaring music from time to time, and neighbors taking showers and its okay. Maybe we've grown harder of hearing, or maybe we've just grown more tolerant and accepting, it's hard to say. What we do know is that we're living a life we love, back where we started and that it isn't something we plan to ever take for granted again.

Life is sweet. We're debt free and living an extremely uncomplicated life. We're back full circle and this time we're loving it just as it is.

Twenty-three

So What Have We Learned From all of This?

- Don't let your belongings own you, own your belongings and make them few.
- Live where you want to live, and do what you want to do—what are you waiting for? Don't wait to start living a life you love.
- Be grateful, be grateful, be grateful.
- Live within your means, purchases on credit equal stress.
- The best way to save money is not to spend it.
- Be kind to animals, they are amazing beings.
- Choose to be happy and live in your present moment, don't worry about what ifs, and don't live in the past or for tomorrow.
- Show love and compassion to all, you've not been crowned as society's judge.
- Practice non-attachment and know that in the words of our yoga teacher Patrick, "the shit sandwich just keeps on coming" so learn to deal with it—that's life.
- Have a sense of adventure. Get a passport and get out there and see the world.
- Always save your best behavior for the ones you love the most.
- Laugh often, especially at yourself.

Lori Colt

Billy the Kid lives happily in San Diego

Made in the USA
Charleston, SC
08 June 2015